THE BIBLE STORYBOOK

For Little Hearts and Big Dreams

*To Penny,
Be Strong and Courageous!
Joshua 1:9*

Joe Bouch

Joseph Bouch

Written by: Joseph Bouch
Illustrations by: Cheryl Amirzadeh, Creative Director 78Madison,
using Adobe Photoshop with generative and manual tools
Design and Layout: Cheryl Amirzadeh

Select illustrations in this book were created using Adobe Photoshop's generative features and have been significantly modified and enhanced through human authorship, including compositing, retouching, and original design input.
All visual content is used under a valid commercial license in accordance with Adobe's terms of use.

Passages in this book are not direct quotations from any formal Bible translation, but are retellings of biblical events in child-friendly language. The wording is original, and not taken word-for-word from any specific Bible version.

First edition
Printed in the United States of America

ISBN (paperback) 978-1-964081-64-9
ISBN (ebook) 978-1-964081-65-6

Dear Dreamer,

Welcome to The Bible Storybook for Little Hearts and Big Dreams*!
This book was written just for you—because your heart is special
to God, and your dreams matter to Him. Every story in these pages
is based on the Bible, God's very own Word. Think of this book as
a companion—a friendly guide to help you understand God's love
letter to the world.*

*As you read, you'll discover how much God loves you, how He
created everything with a purpose, and how He has a big plan for
your life. You'll meet brave heroes like David and Esther, learn from
wise teachers like Solomon and Jesus, and see how God's great love
shines through every story.*

*But these stories aren't just about the past—they're about you, too!
The same God who walked with Noah and cheered on Joshua is
with you today. He wants to help you grow into the big dreams
He's placed in your little heart.*

So, are you ready for the journey?

*Let's step into God's story together. And as you read, remember—
this book points you to the real Bible, where God speaks to every
heart, including yours. You are loved more than you can imagine,
and with God, anything is possible.*

*With love and joy,
Joe Bouch*

In Joe Bouch's opening letter to you, the young dreamer, he says that *The Bible Storybook for Little Hearts and Big Dreams* is a companion to help you understand God's love for you, and it is certainly that. You'll be so glad to have that companion.

But the truth is that it's a good companion for your parents and the older people in your life, too. So, share it with them. Okay?

In C. S. Lewis's dedication to his friend Lucy Barfield, in the first book in his series of Narnia children's stories, he said that she was too old for a child's book, but, when she got older, she could take it down and read it and would enjoy it. In another essay he said that when he was a child, he was embarrassed to read children's books but now, at fifty, he had put away childish things, especially the desire to be grown up.

So, welcome to the Bible, God's message to everyone, everywhere, and for all time. The Bible is kind of like a letter from someone you like and who likes you. But it's more than that. You are going to find that the Bible is not just another religious book. It's interesting, informative, and even fun. But the best part is that it is true, all of it!

Just so you know, there was a time in my life when I didn't believe that the Bible was all true. I'll spare you the details, but I was attending a school in Boston where the Bible was taught as a nice book, but certainly not a true one in the normal understanding of what is true and what isn't. Like C. S. Lewis said, I'm a lot older now and a bit wiser, and I've discovered that the Bible has become my trusted guide to how to live, what's really important, and what life is really about.

I trust that *The Bible Storybook for Little Hearts and Big Dreams* will do that for you, too. In fact, I wish that I had this wonderful book when I was your age. I could have avoided a good deal of pain, a bunch of failures, and so many pitfalls. So, you are fortunate to have this book. It will introduce you to and help you to understand the Bible's truth about everything that's important.

Once you understand what's really important, share it with your friends. Most of them will be so glad you did.

Pastor Steve Brown
Author and Teacher

*"You are loved more than you can imagine, and with God,
anything is possible."*

So concludes the preface to this wonderful new addition to Christian
literature for our children. Can you think of a more important truth our
little ones need to hear as they begin their journey with God? This warm,
faithful summary of every book of the Bible points to the "real Bible" and
helps young hearts trace God's great and loving plan—from the very
beginning—to redeem His people and restore His perfect design for life.
Read it with your precious gifts from God . . . and grow together!

Dr. Pete Alwinson
Pastor/Speaker, FORGE MEN
Orlando, Florida

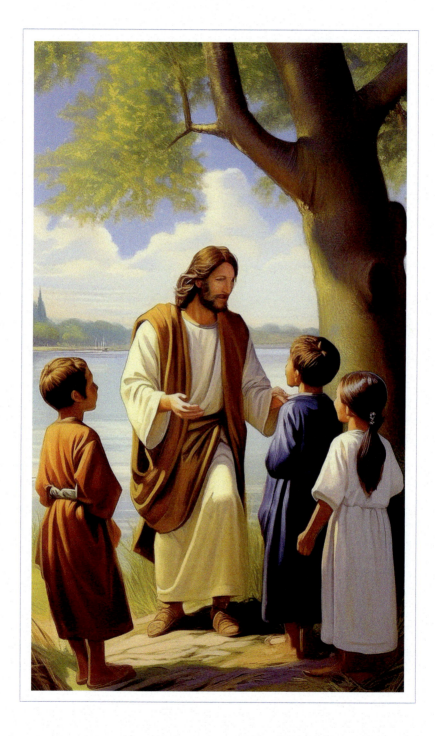

TABLE OF CONTENTS

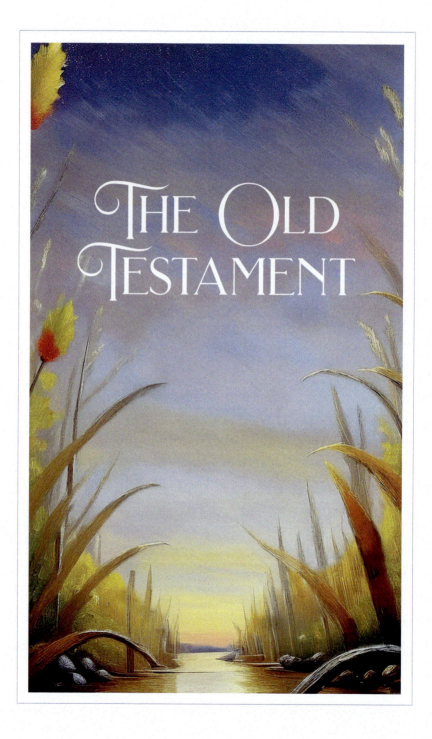

THE OLD TESTAMENT

CHAPTER 1

GENESIS: THE BEGINNING OF EVERYTHING

In the very beginning, there was nothing at all. No trees, no stars, not even a single sound. But then, God spoke. His voice was powerful and loving, like a kind father calling his children. "Let there be light!" He said, and there was light. Bright and warm, it filled the empty space. God smiled because He saw that the light was good.

Then God made the sky and the oceans, the land and the mountains, the trees and the flowers. He filled the seas with fish that swam and the skies with birds that soared. He made lions and sheep, elephants and butterflies, all in their special places. God looked at everything He had made and said, "It is good."

But God wasn't finished yet. He wanted to make someone very special. So, God made a man and a woman, Adam and Eve, in His own image. He gave them eyes to see the bright sun and sparkling stars, ears to hear the chirping birds and rustling leaves, and hearts to love Him and one another. God said, "You are My children. Take care of this beautiful world I've made for you."

Adam and Eve lived in a perfect garden called Eden. It was full of delicious fruit trees and peaceful rivers. God walked with them in the garden, and they were never afraid because they were with Him. "You may eat from any tree in the garden," God said, "except one. The tree of the knowledge of good and evil. If you eat from it, you will surely die." Adam and Eve listened and were happy to obey because they trusted God.

But one day, a sneaky serpent came into the garden. The serpent was crafty and whispered lies to Eve. "Did God really say you can't eat from any tree?" it hissed.

Eve shook her head. "We can eat from every tree but one. If we eat from the tree of the knowledge of good and evil, we will die."

"You won't die," the serpent lied. "If you eat it, you'll be like God, knowing good and evil."

Eve looked at the fruit. It was shiny and beautiful, and she wanted to be wise. So, she took a bite and gave some to Adam, who ate too. As soon as they did, they knew they had disobeyed God. They felt something they had never felt before: shame.

When God came to walk in the garden that evening, Adam and Eve hid. "Where are you?" God called. He already knew what had happened, but He wanted them to come to Him.

Adam said, "We heard You and hid because we're afraid."

"Did you eat from the tree I told you not to eat from?" God asked.

Adam pointed at Eve. "She gave it to me!"

Eve pointed at the serpent. "The serpent tricked me!"

God was sad because Adam and Eve had disobeyed. He told them there would be consequences. Life would be harder now. But God still loved them very much. He promised that one day, He would send a Savior to fix what had gone wrong. Even though Adam and Eve had to leave the garden, God didn't leave them. He cared for them and their children. And His promise of a Savior never changed.

Jesus's Message to You...
This story shows how much God loves you. Even when we make mistakes, He doesn't stop loving us. That's why He sent Me to be your Savior. I came to fix what was broken and to bring you back to God. Always remember, you are loved more than you can imagine!

CHAPTER 2

Exodus: The Great Escape

After Adam and Eve, God's people, the Israelites, were living in Egypt. At first, life was good. But then a new pharaoh, the king of Egypt, came to power. This pharaoh didn't care about God's people. He made them slaves and forced them to work very hard. The Israelites cried out to God for help, and God heard them.

God chose a man named Moses to rescue His people. One day, while Moses was taking care of sheep, he saw something amazing: a bush that was on fire but didn't burn up! Then he heard God's voice. "Moses, I am sending you to Pharaoh to bring My people out of Egypt."

Moses was scared. "Who am I to do this?" he asked.

God said, "I will be with you."

So, Moses went to Pharaoh and said, "Let God's people go!" But Pharaoh said, "No!" He didn't believe in God, and he didn't want to lose his slaves.

God sent ten plagues—punishments for unrighteousness—to show Pharaoh His power. The water in the river turned to blood, frogs covered the land, and hail rained down from the sky. But Pharaoh still said no. Finally, God sent one last plague: every firstborn in Egypt would die. But God told the Israelites to put lamb's blood on their doorposts so that death would pass over their homes. This became known as the first Passover.

That night, Pharaoh finally said, "Go!" The Israelites left quickly. God led them with a pillar of cloud by day and a pillar of fire by night. But Pharaoh changed his mind and chased after them with his army. The Israelites were trapped between Pharaoh's army and the Red Sea.

God told Moses to stretch out his staff over the water. When he did, the sea parted, and the Israelites walked through on dry ground! When Pharaoh's army tried to follow, the waters came back, and they were swept away. God had saved His people.

The Israelites sang a song of thanks to God. They were free! God had shown them that He was their rescuer and that He would always take care of them.

Jesus's Message to You…
Just like My father rescued the Israelites from Egypt, I came to rescue you from sin. When you trust Me, I will always lead you and take care of you. Remember, I am your Savior, and you are never alone!

CHAPTER 3

LEVITICUS: GOD'S RULES OF LOVE

After God rescued the Israelites from Egypt, He wanted to teach them how to live as His special people. They camped at Mount Sinai, where God gave them rules to help them love Him and love each other. These rules are found in the Book of Leviticus.

God said, "Be holy, because I am holy."

Being holy means being close to God and living in a way that pleases Him. God gave the Israelites instructions about how to worship Him, how to treat each other kindly, and even how to take care of the earth and animals. He wanted every part of their lives to show His love and goodness.

One important rule was about loving your neighbor. God said, "Love your neighbor as yourself." This meant helping others, sharing what they needed, and treating everyone with kindness. God also taught the Israelites to be thankful and to give back to Him. They brought offerings of their best animals, grain, and fruit to show their love for God.

Sometimes, the rules were hard to follow, and the Israelites made mistakes. But God had a plan for forgiveness. He told them to bring a lamb or another animal to the priests. The animal would take the punishment for their sin so they could be close to God again. This was a picture of what Jesus would do one day.

When Jesus came, He said, "I didn't come to get rid of God's rules. I came to show you what they mean and to fulfill them." Jesus showed us how to live in God's love perfectly and gave His life so that we could be forgiven forever.

Jesus's Message to You...
God's rules are like a map, guiding you to live in love and kindness. When you make mistakes, remember that I died for you so that you can always be forgiven. Follow Me, and I will help you walk in God's ways. Always love God and love your neighbor!

CHAPTER 4

Numbers: Counting on God

The Israelites were on their way to the land God had promised them, but the journey wasn't easy. They often grumbled and forgot how much God loved them. Still, God was always with them, taking care of their needs.

One day, God told Moses to count all the people. There were so many Israelites, it was like counting stars in the sky! This counting, or census, showed that God was keeping His promise to Abraham to make his family into a great nation.

God also guided the Israelites with a cloud that covered the Tabernacle, a special tent where they worshiped Him. When the cloud moved, the Israelites packed up and followed it. When the cloud stayed, they stayed. It was God's way of saying, "I am leading you."

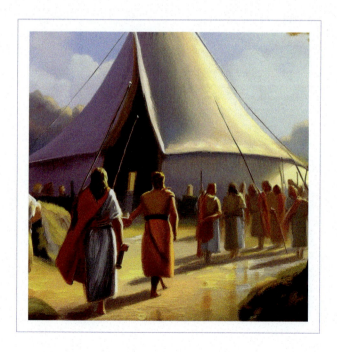

But the Israelites didn't always trust God. When they reached the edge of the promised land, Moses sent twelve men to explore it. They came back with exciting news: "The land is beautiful, flowing with milk and honey!" But ten of the men were afraid. "The people there are giants! We can't defeat them!"

Only two men, Joshua and Caleb, trusted God. "God is with us," they said. "We can do it!" But the Israelites listened to the ten who were afraid. They refused to go into the land, and they even wanted to go back to Egypt.

God was sad that His people didn't trust Him. He said they would have to wander in the wilderness for forty years until a new generation grew up—one that would trust Him completely. Even in their wandering, God took care of them. He gave them manna to eat and water to drink, and their clothes never wore out. He never stopped loving them.

Jesus's Message to You...
Trust in God even when things seem hard or scary. Just like God led the Israelites, I will lead you. Follow Me, and I will show you the way. Remember, you can always count on God!

CHAPTER 5

Deuteronomy: God's Greatest Command

After forty years in the wilderness, the Israelites were finally ready to enter the promised land. But first, Moses spoke to them. He reminded them of everything God had done and the rules He had given them. These words are written in the Book of Deuteronomy.

Moses said, "Listen, Israel: The Lord our God is one. Love the Lord your God with all your heart, with all your soul, and with all your strength." This was the most important command. Moses wanted the Israelites to always remember to love and obey God.

Moses told the people to teach God's words to their children. "Talk about them at home and when you walk along the road, when you lie down and when you get up. Write them on your doors and gates." Moses wanted everyone to know and love God.

Before the Israelites entered the land, Moses said, "Choose life by loving the Lord your God, obeying Him, and holding fast to Him." Then Moses climbed a mountain, and God took him to heaven. Joshua became the new leader of the Israelites, and he would help them trust God as they entered the promised land.

Jesus's Message to You…
Loving God with all your heart is the most important thing you can do. I came to show you how much God loves you and to help you love Him too. Always remember, God's love for you never ends!

CHAPTER 6

JOSHUA: BEING BRAVE AND STRONG

The Israelites finally crossed into the promised land, but it wasn't empty. Other people lived there, and they didn't want to leave. God told Joshua, "Be strong and courageous. I will be with you wherever you go."

The first city they came to was Jericho, which had big, strong walls. God gave Joshua special instructions. "March around the city once a day for six days. On the seventh day, march around it seven times, then have the priests blow their trumpets and the people shout."

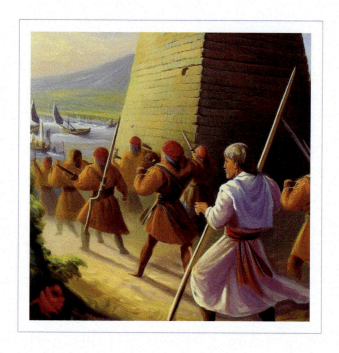

Joshua and the Israelites obeyed. On the seventh day, when they shouted, the walls of Jericho came tumbling down! The Israelites trusted God, and He gave them victory.

As they moved through the land, Joshua reminded the people to obey God and worship Him alone. He said, "Choose this day whom you will serve. As for me and my house, we will serve the Lord."

Jesus's Message to You...
Trust God like Joshua did. Be brave and strong, knowing that I am with you. When you face challenges, remember that God is your helper and protector. Follow Him, and you will always have His strength!

CHAPTER 7

Judges: God's Helpers

After Joshua died, the Israelites forgot to follow God. They started doing what was wrong and worshiping false gods. This made their lives very hard. But whenever they cried out to God, He sent helpers called judges to rescue them.

One of the judges was Deborah. She was wise and brave, and she helped the Israelites win a big battle. Another judge was Gideon. He was scared at first, but God told him, "I will be with you." Gideon led a tiny army against a big enemy, and they won because God fought for them.

The strongest judge was Samson. God gave him incredible strength to fight Israel's enemies. But Samson made mistakes and didn't always obey God. When he asked God for help, God gave him strength one last time to defeat the enemy.

The judges weren't perfect, but God used them to save His people and remind them to follow Him.

Jesus's Message to You...
Even when you make mistakes, God can still use you to do great things. Trust in Me, and I will always show you the way.

CHAPTER 8

Ruth: A Big Decision

In the land of Israel, there was a famine. A woman named Naomi and her family moved to a faraway land called Moab to find food. But while they were there, Naomi's husband and two sons died. Naomi was very sad. All she had left were her two daughters-in-law, Orpah and Ruth.

Naomi decided to go back to Israel because she heard the famine was over. She told Orpah and Ruth, "You should go back to your families. You have been kind to me, but I have nothing to give you."

Orpah hugged Naomi and went back home, but Ruth said, "I won't leave you! Where you go, I will go. Your people will be my people, and your God will be my God." Ruth loved Naomi and wanted to stay with her.

So, Ruth and Naomi went to Bethlehem, Naomi's hometown. It was harvesting time, and Ruth worked in the fields, picking up leftover grain so they could have food. The field belonged to a kind man named Boaz. When Boaz saw Ruth, he heard about how she had cared for Naomi. He told his workers to leave extra grain for her and made sure she was safe.

Boaz and Ruth grew to care for each other. Boaz followed God's laws and became Ruth's family protector. Soon, they were married! God blessed them with a son named Obed, who became the grandfather of King David. Ruth's love and faithfulness showed how God brings hope even in hard times.

Jesus's Message to You…
Ruth's story reminds us to be kind, faithful, and trust in God.
Just like Ruth cared for Naomi, I care for you. When you
trust in Me, I will guide you and bring blessings into your
life. Always remember, God has a special plan for you!

CHAPTER 9

1 Samuel: Trusting God's Plan

A man named Samuel was a prophet and judge over Israel. Israel was a special nation that God chose to be His people. But for many years, they didn't have a king like other nations. Instead, they were led by judges, and Samuel was one of them. He loved God and helped the people of Israel follow Him. The story of 1 Samuel shows how God chose a king for His people and how He was always in control of Israel's future.

At the beginning of the book, we learn about a woman named Hannah. She was sad because she didn't have any children, and she prayed to God with all her heart, asking for a son. Hannah promised that if God gave her a son, she would dedicate him to God's service for his whole life. God answered her prayer and gave her a son named Samuel. True to her word, Hannah brought Samuel to the temple when he was old enough to serve God, and Samuel grew up in God's house, learning to listen to God's voice.

One night, when Samuel was still young, God called out to him. At first, Samuel didn't know it was God's voice, so he ran to Eli, the priest, thinking it was Eli calling him. But Eli told him to go back to bed. This happened three times until Eli realized that it was God calling Samuel. Eli told Samuel to answer, "Speak, Lord, for Your servant is listening." And when Samuel did, God spoke to him, giving him a message for Israel. From then on, Samuel became known as a prophet who faithfully spoke God's words to the people.

As Samuel grew older, the people of Israel asked for a king, because they wanted to be like other nations. This upset Samuel, but God told him, "It is not you they have rejected, but they have rejected Me as their king." God allowed them to have a king, but He warned them that having a king would bring trouble. God told Samuel to anoint a man named Saul as the first king of Israel.

Saul was tall and handsome, but he was not always faithful to God. At first, Saul started off well, leading Israel in battles and obeying God's commands. But soon, Saul began to disobey God, making decisions based on his own ideas instead of listening to God's instructions. God became very disappointed with Saul and told Samuel that He was going to choose a new king to replace him.

God told Samuel to go to the house of a man named Jesse, because one of his sons was going to be the new king. When Samuel arrived, he saw Jesse's oldest son, Eliab, and thought, "Surely this is the one God has chosen!" But God told Samuel, "Do not consider his appearance or his height, for I have rejected him. The Lord does not look at the things people look at. People look at the outward appearance, but the Lord looks at the heart." One by one, Jesse's sons passed before Samuel, but God told Samuel that none of them were the one. Finally, Jesse called for his youngest son, David, who was out in the fields taking care of the sheep. When David came, God told Samuel, "Rise and anoint him; this is the one." So, Samuel anointed David, and from that day on, God's Spirit was with him.

David became a mighty warrior and eventually the king of Israel, but not before facing many challenges. One of the most famous stories in 1 Samuel is how David defeated the giant Goliath. While everyone else was afraid of the giant, David trusted in God and knew that God would help him. With just a sling and a stone, David defeated Goliath, showing that when we trust God, we can overcome anything.

Throughout the story of 1 Samuel, we see how God works in surprising ways, choosing leaders based on their hearts, not their outward appearances. Even when things seemed difficult, God was in control, and He always had a plan for His people. Samuel, Saul, and David all had different paths, but God used them in His great plan for Israel.

Jesus's Message to You...
Remember that I see your heart, not just what is on the outside. Like David, you can trust in Me even when things seem impossible. I am always with you, and I have a plan for you, just like I had a plan for Samuel and David. When you listen to My voice and follow My ways, I will help you be brave and strong. Trust in Me, for I am with you always!

CHAPTER 10

2 Samuel: God's Promise and King David's Reign

After King Saul died, God made David the king of Israel. David had been chosen by God when he was just a young shepherd, and now, as king, he would lead God's people. The story of 2 Samuel shows how David became a great king, made some mistakes, and learned about God's mercy and faithfulness.

At the beginning of 2 Samuel, David hears about the death of Saul and his friend Jonathan. Even though Saul had been his enemy, David was very sad. He wrote a song to honor Saul and Jonathan, showing that even when things didn't go well between them, David loved them as part of God's plan. David's heart was full of love and respect for those who had served God, and he knew that God had a special plan for all people.

When David became king, he made Jerusalem his capital city, and it became a very important place. David wanted to bring the Ark of the Covenant to Jerusalem because it was a symbol of God's presence among His people. But when David tried to bring the Ark, something went wrong, and one of David's men, Uzzah, touched the Ark and died. David was afraid, but he learned that following God's commands is very important, and he made sure to do things the right way. Finally, the Ark was brought into Jerusalem, and David danced before the Lord with all his might, praising God for His goodness.

God made a special promise to David. He told David that He would build a house for him, meaning that David's family would always have a king on the throne of Israel. This was the promise of a king from David's family who would rule forever, and God was speaking about Jesus, who would come many years later.

David was a great king, but he also made mistakes. One of the most serious mistakes was when David sinned with Bathsheba, the wife of one of his soldiers, Uriah. David saw Bathsheba, and instead of making a good choice, he did something very wrong. He tried to cover up his sin by having Uriah killed in battle, but God sent the prophet Nathan to confront David. David repented, asking God for forgiveness, and God forgave him, but there were still consequences for his actions. David learned that even though God forgives us when we sin, sin still has effects on our lives and the lives of others.

David's reign as king wasn't always easy. There were many wars and battles, and even some of his own family members rebelled against him. His son Absalom tried to take over the throne, and David had to flee from his own city. But even during the hard times, David trusted in God and asked for His help. In the end, Absalom was defeated, and David returned to Jerusalem as king. Through it all, David learned to rely on God's strength, wisdom, and mercy.

At the end of 2 Samuel, David praises God for His faithfulness and reflects on the many ways God has blessed him. David knew that everything he had was from God, and he promised to build a house for God, a temple, though it would be his son Solomon who would do it.

Jesus's Message to You...

Like David, you may make mistakes, but remember that God is always ready to forgive you when you ask. Just like David, you can trust God even when things are tough. He has a plan for you and will always be with you. And remember, I am the King that God promised would come from David's family, and I am the King who will never leave you. Trust in God, follow His ways, and know that He will always love you!

CHAPTER 11

1 Kings: The Rise of Kings

After King David's reign, his son Solomon became the king of Israel. The story of 1 Kings tells how Solomon built a magnificent temple for God, how Israel prospered under his leadership, and how the kingdom eventually split into two after Solomon's death. This book also shows how God worked through the kings of Israel, both good and bad, and how He was always faithful to His people.

At the beginning of 1 Kings, David was getting old, and his son Solomon was anointed as the new king. David gave Solomon wise advice, urging him to follow God's commands and be faithful to Him. Solomon, at first, was known for his wisdom. One of the most famous stories of Solomon's wisdom is when two women came to him, both claiming to be the mother of the same baby. Solomon, knowing that only a true mother would care for her child, suggested cutting the baby in half and giving each woman a part. The real mother immediately offered to give up her claim to save the child's life, and Solomon knew she was the true mother. This story showed how wise and just Solomon was, and people came from all over to hear his wisdom.

Solomon also built a beautiful temple for God in Jerusalem, fulfilling the promise that David had made to God. The temple was a place where the people could worship God, and it was filled with gold, precious stones, and fine wood. When the temple was finished, Solomon prayed to God, asking Him to bless the temple and the people of Israel. God's presence filled the temple in a way that was so powerful that the priests couldn't even stand to minister. God told Solomon that if the people of Israel remained faithful to Him, He would bless them, but if they turned away, He would punish them.

During Solomon's reign, Israel became a powerful and wealthy nation. Solomon's wisdom was admired by many, and the people lived in peace. But even though Solomon started off well, he began to make some unwise decisions. He married many foreign women and allowed them to bring their idols and false gods into Israel. Eventually, Solomon's heart turned away from God, and he began to worship these idols. God became angry with Solomon and told him that, because of his disobedience, the kingdom would be divided after his death.

After Solomon died, his son Rehoboam became king. However, Rehoboam made a foolish choice by refusing to listen to the older advisors who urged him to be kind to the people. Instead, he listened to his younger friends, who told him to be harsh and demanding. Because of this, ten of the twelve tribes of Israel rebelled and chose a new king, Jeroboam, who led the northern kingdom. Rehoboam remained king over the southern kingdom, which was called Judah.

This division of Israel into two kingdoms—Israel in the north and Judah in the south—caused many problems. Both kingdoms had their share of good and bad kings. Some kings were faithful to God, but many led the people into idolatry and sin. One of the most wicked kings of Israel was Ahab, who married Jezebel and allowed her to lead Israel into worshiping false gods, especially Baal. The prophet Elijah spoke out against Ahab and Jezebel, calling the people to return to God. God performed amazing miracles through Elijah, including sending fire from heaven to prove that He alone was the true God.

At the end of 1 Kings, we see how God remained faithful even in the midst of a divided and rebellious nation. God sent prophets like Elijah and Elisha to remind the people of His love and call them to repentance. Though Israel was far from perfect, God was still working to bring His people back to Himself.

Jesus's Message to You...
Just like Solomon, you can ask Me for wisdom to help you make good choices. When you trust in Me, I will help you make the right choices and to follow God's ways, just like the prophets helped the people in the past. God is always faithful, and His love never changes!

CHAPTER 12

2 Kings: The Rise and Fall of Kings

The story of 2 Kings continues the journey of Israel and Judah, showing how the kingdoms of Israel and Judah had many kings—some who followed God, and others who turned away from Him. Through all the ups and downs, God remained faithful to His promises, sending prophets to guide and warn the people. But, because the kings and people often ignored God's Word, both kingdoms faced destruction.

At the beginning of 2 Kings, we learn about the end of King David's family line in Judah. After the great prophet Elijah went to heaven, his servant Elisha took his place as a prophet of God. Elisha performed many miracles, like healing the sick, providing for the poor, and even raising the dead. He reminded the people of Israel to turn back to God and stop worshiping idols. Even though Elisha did great things by God's power, the people didn't always listen to God's message.

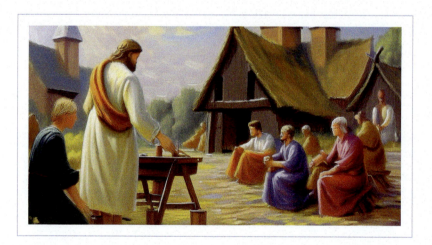

In Israel, the northern kingdom, there were many kings who did not follow God. They worshiped idols and did evil in God's eyes. One of the most wicked kings was Ahab, and his wife Jezebel. They led Israel away from God, and God sent Elijah to speak against them.

Eventually, Elijah was taken up to heaven, and Elisha continued to carry out God's work. But the people of Israel didn't change their ways, and they suffered because of it.

In Judah, the southern kingdom, there were some kings who loved God, like King Hezekiah and King Josiah. These kings led reforms, tearing down idols and turning the people back to God. But even in Judah, many kings did not follow God, and their hearts grew hard. Despite the good kings, the people of Judah also turned away from God, and they were eventually conquered by the Babylonians, who took them into exile.

The fall of Israel and Judah was a result of the people repeatedly turning away from God and worshiping idols. They had forgotten to trust in God alone, and instead, they relied on their own strength and the false gods of other nations. God had warned them again and again through the prophets, but the people didn't listen. As a result, God allowed their enemies to defeat them. Israel, the northern kingdom, was conquered by Assyria, and Judah, the southern kingdom, was conquered by Babylon. Both kingdoms were taken into exile, but God promised to one day bring His people back to the land.

At the end of 2 Kings, we see that God's judgment had come upon Israel and Judah because they had turned away from Him. But even in the midst of judgment, God remained faithful to His promises. He didn't forget His people, and He promised that one day He would restore them. The story of 2 Kings reminds us that God's Word is serious, and that we must always listen to Him, trust Him, and follow His ways.

Jesus's Message to You…
Even when the people of Israel and Judah made bad choices, My Father was always faithful. He loves you, and He promises to forgive you when you ask. Like the prophets, God will speak to our hearts, telling us to trust in Him and to follow His ways.

CHAPTER 13

1 Chronicles: God's Promise to David

After the time of King David, the people of Israel wanted to remember all that God had done for them. The Book of 1 Chronicles focuses on the history of Israel, especially the reign of King David. It reminds the people that God is faithful and always keeps His promises. This book also highlights the importance of worshiping God and trusting in Him, as David did with all his heart.

At the beginning of 1 Chronicles, we read about the family tree of Adam all the way down to King David. This list of names helps us see how God worked through many generations to bring His people together. Even though there were many people who lived before David, God had a plan for Israel, and David was part of that plan.

David, the shepherd boy who became king, is the central figure in 1 Chronicles. His story shows how God used an ordinary man, with a heart that loved God, to do extraordinary things. When David became king, he united Israel and made Jerusalem the capital city. He wanted to build a temple for God, a place where the people could worship God in a special way. However, God told David that he would not be the one to build the temple, but his son Solomon would.

Even though David couldn't build the temple, he gathered everything needed for the construction, including gold, silver, and precious stones, to make sure Solomon would have everything he needed.

David also led the people of Israel in worship. He organized the Levites and priests to sing and play music in the temple, so that the people could praise God. David wrote many of the psalms that are still sung today—songs that express his love for God, his trust in God, and his desire to follow God's will. David's heart was full of worship, and he wanted all of Israel to worship God too.

As we read through 1 Chronicles, we see that David was a great king who faced many challenges. He fought battles, made mistakes, and had times when he trusted God and other times when he failed. But through it all, David knew that God was faithful, and he always turned back to God in repentance. Even when David sinned, God forgave him and restored him. David's life teaches us that God is gracious and merciful, and that He always welcomes us back when we turn to Him.

At the end of 1 Chronicles, David prepares for the future. He speaks to the people, reminding them of God's faithfulness and encouraging them to stay true to God. He passes the responsibility of building the temple to his son Solomon, and he asks the people to support Solomon as their new king. David knows that God's promises will continue through Solomon and that God will always be with His people.

Jesus's Message to You…
David worshiped God and wanted to make sure that everyone knew how good God is. You can do the same by loving God, singing songs of praise, and trusting that God has a plan for you. Just like God was faithful to David, He will always be faithful to you, and He will help you follow Him every day.

CHAPTER 14

2 Chronicles: The Building of the Temple

After King David's reign, his son Solomon became the king of Israel. The story of 2 Chronicles begins with Solomon's reign, focusing on how God used him to build a beautiful temple in Jerusalem. The temple would be a place where God's people could worship Him and offer sacrifices. It was a special symbol of God's presence with them. Through Solomon, God's promises were being fulfilled.

In the beginning of 2 Chronicles, Solomon asks God for wisdom. God was pleased with Solomon's request because instead of asking for riches or power, Solomon wanted to be a wise king who could lead God's people well. God granted Solomon wisdom, and he became known as the wisest king who ever lived. Solomon also built the magnificent temple, following God's instructions carefully. This temple was a place where the Israelites could meet with God, and it showed how God had chosen to dwell with His people.

Throughout 2 Chronicles, we read about the kings of Judah, the southern kingdom. Some of the kings were good and followed God, while others turned away from Him and worshiped idols. When the kings followed God and led the people in worship, things went well for Judah.

But when the kings turned away from God, they faced trouble and defeat. The people were warned by prophets to repent and return to God, but they often ignored His message.

One of the best kings in Judah's history was King Hezekiah. Hezekiah trusted in God and led the people to remove idols and restore proper worship in the temple. Hezekiah even prayed to God for help when the Assyrians, a powerful enemy, threatened Judah. God answered his prayer by delivering Judah from the Assyrians and protecting the city.

Another great king was Josiah. He was just a young boy when he became king, but he loved God with all his heart. Josiah discovered God's Word in the temple, and when he read it, he realized how far the people had turned away from God. He led Judah in a great reform, tearing down idols and renewing the covenant with God. Under Josiah's leadership, the people returned to worshiping God as they should.

Sadly, after Josiah, many of the kings of Judah were wicked and did not follow God. They ignored God's commands and continued to worship idols. God warned them through the prophets, but they did not listen. Eventually, Judah was defeated by Babylon, and the people were taken into exile. Even though they faced judgment, God's promises were still true. He had said that one day, He would bring His people back to their land, and He would continue to work out His plan of salvation.

At the end of 2 Chronicles, we see the fall of Judah, but we also see a glimmer of hope. The book ends with the decree of the Persian king, Cyrus, who allowed the people of Judah to return to their land and rebuild the temple. Even though they were taken into exile because of their disobedience, God's mercy was greater, and He gave them a chance to rebuild and restore their relationship with Him.

Jesus's Message to You...
We can trust that God will help you, just like He helped Hezekiah and Josiah. And when you mess up, God is always ready to forgive you and help you start fresh. Remember, God has a plan for you, and He will never leave you!

CHAPTER 15

EZRA: RETURNING TO REBUILD GOD'S HOUSE

The people of Israel had been taken far away from their home to a place called Babylon. They were sad because they couldn't live in their city, and most of all, the beautiful temple where they worshiped God was destroyed. But after many years, the king of Persia, King Cyrus, allowed the Israelites to return to their land and rebuild God's house, the temple.

One of the leaders who helped them on this journey was a man named Ezra. Ezra was a priest who loved God and studied His Word. He knew how important it was to follow God's teachings and help the people return to worshiping God the right way. Ezra's heart was filled with excitement because God had allowed him to lead the people back to their home, and he was ready to help them rebuild the temple.

When Ezra arrived in Jerusalem, the people began the hard work of rebuilding God's house. They worked together, gathering the stones, and restoring what had been broken. But the journey was not easy. There were people who didn't want to see the temple rebuilt, and they tried to stop the work. Ezra didn't let the enemies distract him. He trusted that God was with him and kept moving forward with the rebuilding.

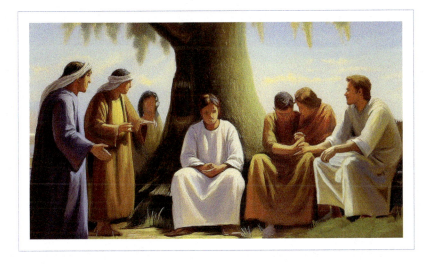

Ezra also knew that something very important had to happen before the people could truly be close to God again. He began reading and teaching God's Word to the people. He reminded them of the laws God had given them and how they needed to live in a way that honored God. The people listened to Ezra and prayed for God to forgive them for their mistakes. They promised to follow God's commands.

God was pleased with Ezra's leadership, and the temple was completed. The people rejoiced and celebrated because they knew that they were once again able to worship God in His holy house. Ezra's heart was full of joy because he had helped the people turn back to God, and they were once again united in worship.

Jesus's Message to You…
Ezra's story shows that when you work together and trust God, you can overcome challenges. He is with you in every task. Keep building your faith and helping others. Together, we can do amazing things for God!

CHAPTER 16

NEHEMIAH: BUILDING WITH GOD'S HELP

A long time ago, in the city of Jerusalem, the walls were broken down, and the people there felt unsafe and sad. The city had been destroyed, and the people didn't have strong walls to protect them. They longed for the day when the city would be safe and whole again.

Nehemiah was a man who lived far away from Jerusalem, serving as a cupbearer to the king in a place called Persia. He had a good job, but one day, he heard about how Jerusalem was still in ruins. Dejected, he prayed to God, asking for help. Nehemiah knew that God had a plan for His people, and he wanted to be part of it.

After Nehemiah prayed, something amazing happened. The king noticed that Nehemiah was sad and asked him what was wrong.

Nehemiah told the king about the broken walls of Jerusalem and how he wanted to rebuild them. The king was kind and gave Nehemiah everything he needed to go back to Jerusalem and fix the walls.

Nehemiah traveled to Jerusalem and began to organize the people to rebuild the city's walls. But there were some people who didn't want to see Jerusalem become strong again. They made fun of Nehemiah and tried to stop the work. Nehemiah didn't give up, though. He knew that God was with him, so he encouraged the people to keep working and trust God.

Nehemiah's leadership was amazing. He made sure that everyone worked together, and even when the enemies tried to stop them, the people kept building the walls. They worked day and night, trusting that God would protect them and help them finish the job. After much hard work, the walls were finally finished! The people of Jerusalem were so happy. They praised God for helping them rebuild the city, and they knew that with God's strength, anything was possible.

Nehemiah's story teaches us that with God's help, we can accomplish big things, even when they seem impossible. He trusted in God's plan, worked hard, and didn't give up, no matter how tough things got. So, the next time you face something big or difficult, remember Nehemiah. He trusted God, worked hard, and didn't give up. With God's help, you can do amazing things too!

Jesus's Message to You...
Nehemiah's story reminds us that prayer and teamwork are powerful. When you face challenges, remember that I am with you. Be brave and keep going, because I will help you succeed!

CHAPTER 17

ESTHER: GOD HAS A PLAN FOR YOU

There was a young woman named Esther who lived in a kingdom called Persia. She was a Jewish girl, and her family had been taken far away from their home. One day, something special happened that would change Esther's life forever. The king of Persia, King Xerxes, decided he needed a new queen. He sent out word for all the young women in the kingdom to come to the palace so he could choose one to be his queen.

Esther was beautiful, but there was something even more special about her—she trusted God and was brave. She didn't tell the king or anyone else that she was Jewish, because she knew that it was important to keep that secret at the right time. Esther was chosen to be the queen of Persia, and she lived in the palace with the king.

But one day, something very scary happened. The king's evil helper, Haman, wanted to hurt all the Jewish people in the kingdom. He planned to have them killed. When Esther's cousin, Mordecai, found out about this plan, he sent a message to Esther. He told her, "You were chosen to be queen for a reason. You might be the only one who can save the Jewish people."

At first, Esther was afraid. She knew that the king had the power to do anything, and she couldn't go to him without being called. But Mordecai reminded her, "Who knows, maybe you became queen for such a time as this." Esther prayed, asking God for help. Then she made a brave decision. She went to the king and asked him to save her people.

The king was surprised to see her, but he welcomed her. Esther invited the king and Haman to a special dinner, and at the dinner, she told the king about Haman's evil plan. The king was angry and ordered that Haman be stopped. Because of Esther's courage and God's help, the Jewish people were saved!

Esther's story shows us that even when things seem scary, God has a plan for us. Esther was just a young girl, but God used her to save many people. She was brave, trusted God, and knew that God could use her, no matter how difficult the situation seemed. So, the next time you feel like you can't do something, remember Esther. She was brave and trusted that God had a plan for her, and God used her to save an entire people. You can trust that God has a plan for you too.

Jesus's Message to You...
Esther's story shows that God has a purpose for you, just as He did for her. Be brave and trust in Me, because I will help you do what is right. Remember, you are part of God's amazing plan!

CHAPTER 18

JOB: TRUSTING GOD THROUGH HARD TIMES

Job was a very good man who loved God and did his best to live in a way that pleased Him. Job had a big family, many friends, and lots of animals. He was blessed in every way, and he was known for being a wise and kind person. But one day, everything in Job's life changed.

Job lost everything. His animals were taken away, his house was destroyed, and even his children died. Job was very sad and didn't understand why all these terrible things were happening to him. Even though Job was sad, he never blamed God. He said, "The Lord gave, and the Lord has taken away; may the name of the Lord be praised." Job still trusted that God knew what was best.

Job's friends came to visit him. They saw how down and sick he was, and they sat with him. But soon, they started talking and telling Job that all these bad things must have happened because he did something wrong. They said, "Maybe you sinned against God." But Job knew that he hadn't done anything to deserve what was happening. He asked, "Why, God, are You letting this happen to me?"

Even though Job didn't understand, he continued to trust in God. He never gave up. Finally, God spoke to Job. God reminded Job that He is the Creator of everything—the earth, the stars, the oceans, and the animals. He told Job that we cannot always understand everything that happens, but God is wise and knows what is best.

Job realized that God is in control, even when things are hard. He said, "I know that You can do all things; no purpose of Yours can be thwarted." Job trusted that God would take care of him no matter what. And in the end, God blessed Job again, giving him a new family, more animals, and a long life full of peace.

The story of Job teaches us that it's okay to feel sad or confused, but we can always trust that God is in control. Sometimes bad things happen, but that doesn't mean God has forgotten us. We can keep trusting God, even when we don't understand why things are happening.

Jesus's Message to You...
Job's story teaches us to trust God, no matter what happens. When life feels hard, remember that I am with you and will never leave you. I will bring you peace and hope, just as God did for Job.

CHAPTER 19

PSALMS: SONGS OF PRAISE AND PRAYER

There was a man named David who loved God with all his heart. He wrote many songs and prayers to God, and these were collected in a book called Psalms. Psalms is a special book in the Bible, filled with songs, praises, and prayers that express every feeling we could ever have.

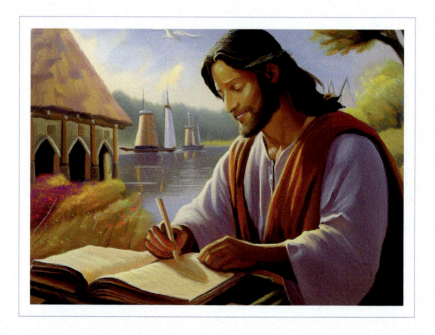

Sometimes, David sang songs of joy because he felt thankful and happy. He praised God for His goodness, saying things like, "The Lord is my shepherd; I shall not want," meaning that God takes care of him and provides for all his needs.

Other times, David sang sad songs when he was feeling afraid or sad. He cried out to God, saying, "Why, Lord, do You stand far off? Why do You hide Yourself in times of trouble?" Even when David was sad, he knew that God would hear his prayers and be with him through tough times.

David also wrote songs to remind himself and others that God is always with them. He knew that God is strong and mighty. He said, "The Lord is my light and my salvation—whom shall I fear? The Lord is the stronghold of my life—of whom shall I be afraid?" David trusted that no matter what happened, God would protect him and help him.

One of the most famous psalms is Psalm 23, where David talks about how God leads him like a shepherd guides his sheep. "The Lord is my shepherd; I shall not want. He makes me lie down in green pastures. He leads me beside still waters. He restores my soul." David trusted God to lead him to safety and peace.

Jesus's Message to You...
The Psalms remind us we can praise God for His goodness and thank Him for His care. God is with us through every emotion—whether we're happy, sad, or afraid, and we can always talk to God and know that He listens to our prayers.

CHAPTER 20

PROVERBS: WISDOM FOR LIFE

There was a king named Solomon, and he was known for being very wise. People came from far and wide just to hear him speak. Solomon wrote a book called Proverbs to help people live good lives and make wise choices. The book is full of short, helpful sayings that can guide us every day, no matter how old we are.

Solomon knew that life could be tricky.

Sometimes we don't know what to do or which choice is best. But he wanted everyone to know that wisdom—making choices that honor God—is the key to living a happy and successful life.

The Book of Proverbs teaches us many things, including:

- **The importance of wisdom:**
  Wisdom is more valuable than gold or silver! Solomon said, "Wisdom is better than rubies, and nothing you desire can compare with her." When we seek wisdom, we can make good decisions that help us grow closer to God.
- **Listening to God:**
  Solomon says, "Trust in the Lord with all your heart and lean not on your own understanding." This means we should always look to God for guidance, especially when we're unsure about what to do.
- **Choosing good friends:**
  Solomon reminds us that the people we spend time with can help or hurt us. "Walk with the wise and become wise, for a companion of fools suffers harm." It's important to choose friends who encourage us to do what's right and follow God.
- **Being kind and honest:**
  A wise person is kind, gentle, and truthful. "The wise in heart accept commands, but a chattering fool comes to ruin." It's better to speak kindly and tell the truth, even when it's hard.
- **Living with a joyful heart:**
  Solomon also teaches us that a happy heart is a wise heart. "A cheerful heart is good medicine, but a crushed spirit dries up the bones." Being kind, loving, and thankful makes our lives much brighter!

One of the most famous verses in Proverbs is, "The fear of the Lord is the beginning of wisdom." This means that when we respect and honor God, we're on the right path to making wise choices.

So, the next time you have a big decision to make or need guidance, remember the Proverbs and turn to God for wisdom. He will help you make the right choices and live a life that honors Him.

Jesus's Message to You...
Proverbs teaches you how to make good choices. Listen to My words, for I am the source of all wisdom. When you trust and follow Me, I will help you live a life that pleases God and blesses others.

CHAPTER 21

ECCLESIASTES: FINDING JOY IN GOD'S PURPOSE

In this book, we find that King Solomon had everything anyone could want—riches, fame, wisdom, and power. But one day, he sat down and thought, "What is the purpose of life? Why do we do all these things? What really makes us happy?"

Solomon looked at the world and saw that people were always working hard to get more things. They built big houses, earned lots of money, and sought after fun and pleasure, but it all seemed to be temporary. He called it "chasing after the wind"—because no matter how hard you chase, you can never catch it.

He asked big questions, like:

- What's the point of working hard if it doesn't last?
- What good is it to be rich if you can't take your wealth with you when you die?
- Why do we suffer, and what can we do about it?

But even though Solomon saw how many things in life seemed empty, he didn't give up. He reminded himself—and us—that the real purpose of life is to enjoy the simple gifts God gives us. Solomon said, "There is nothing better than to eat, drink, and find satisfaction in your work. This is a gift from God."

Solomon also said that life is full of seasons—sometimes things go well, and sometimes they don't. But no matter what happens, we can trust that God is in control and has a plan for everything. "There is a time for everything," Solomon said, "a time to be born and a time to die, a time to cry and a time to laugh."

In the end, Solomon reminded us that we should always remember God, because He made everything and knows what's best for us. Solomon said, "Fear God and keep His commandments, for this is the whole duty of man."

Ecclesiastes teaches us life has many ups and downs, but we can find joy in God's gifts to us. We don't have to chase after things that won't last. What really matters is loving God and enjoying the simple things in life. God is in control of everything, and we can trust His plan.

Jesus's Message to You…
Ecclesiastes shows that life without God feels empty, but with Me, your life is full of purpose and joy. Follow Me, and I will lead you to a life that matters forever.

CHAPTER 22

SONG OF SOLOMON: GOD'S LOVE FOR US

There was a beautiful song called the Song of Solomon. It wasn't just a song about two people in love, but it also showed how much God loves His people. This song talks about the love between a husband and a wife, but it also helps us understand how deep and wonderful God's love is for us.

In this beautiful poem, a young woman, called the Shulammite, and her beloved speak to each other. They admire each other's beauty, and they express their love for one another. The woman says to her beloved, "You are my love, and I am yours," and the man tells her, "How delightful you are, my love!" Their words are full of joy and tenderness, just like a couple who deeply cares for each other.

But the Song of Solomon isn't only about romantic love. It teaches us about how much God loves us. God's love is pure and beautiful, like the love between the man and woman in the song. His love is deep, unchanging, and faithful, no matter what.

In fact, the song uses beautiful pictures of love to show how much God cherishes His people. It talks about the way He sees us as precious and beautiful, like a garden full of wonderful flowers and fragrant spices. God says to His people, "You are beautiful, My love, and I delight in you!"

The Song of Solomon also reminds us that God's love is strong. It's a love that nothing can take away. In one part of the song, the woman says, "Love is as strong as death, and its jealousy is as fierce as the grave." God's love is powerful, and it will never end.

The Song of Solomon is a celebration of love. It teaches us that God's love for us is beautiful, deep, and never-ending. We can find joy in knowing that God sees us as His precious and beloved children. True love, like God's love, is strong and unshakeable.

Jesus's Message to You…
Song of Solomon shows how deeply I love you. I gave My life for you because you are precious to Me. Always remember, you are loved more than you can imagine.

CHAPTER 23

Isaiah: A Vision of God's Amazing Love

There was a prophet named Isaiah. He lived in a time when the people of Israel had turned away from God. They were doing bad things, and many of them didn't listen to God's messages. But Isaiah loved God deeply, and he knew God had something important to say to the people.

One day, Isaiah had an amazing vision. He saw God sitting on a throne, high and mighty, surrounded by angels singing, "Holy, holy, holy is the Lord Almighty!" The whole room was filled with God's glory, and everything trembled in His presence.

Isaiah was so amazed by what he saw, but he also felt very small. "I am not worthy to be in Your presence, Lord," he said. "I am a sinner."

But God sent one of the angels to Isaiah with a burning coal. The angel touched it to Isaiah's lips and said, "Your sins are forgiven. Now you are clean."

Then, God asked, "Whom shall I send to tell My people what they need to know?" And Isaiah replied, "Here am I, Lord. Send me!"

Isaiah became God's messenger. He had to tell the people many hard things, like how they needed to turn away from their sinful ways and return to God. He warned them that if they didn't change, they would face consequences. But Isaiah also brought them words of hope.

Isaiah told the people about a special servant who would come one day. This servant would bring salvation to everyone, not just Israel. He would be someone who would suffer for the sins of the world and bring healing to the brokenhearted. This servant was Jesus, the Messiah!

One of the most famous verses from Isaiah says, "The Lord Himself will give you a sign: the virgin will conceive and give birth to a son, and will call him Immanuel, which means 'God with us.'" Isaiah was telling the people that God would send His Son to be with them and save them from their sins.

Isaiah's story teaches us that God is holy and powerful, and we should honor Him. Even when we make mistakes, God forgives us and gives us a fresh start. God's plan for salvation is for everyone, and He sent Jesus to be our Savior.

Jesus's Message to You…
Isaiah's words were about Me! I came to be your Savior because I love you so much. Trust in Me, and I will guide you, forgive you, and give you peace. You are part of My great plan of love and hope.

CHAPTER 24

JEREMIAH: GOD'S CALL TO STAND STRONG

There was a prophet named Jeremiah. He was just a young boy when God called him to do something very important: to tell the people of Judah that they needed to change their ways. But it wasn't an easy job. The people didn't want to listen to Jeremiah's message, and they kept doing bad things.

God told Jeremiah, "I have chosen you to speak My words, even though it will be hard. Don't be afraid, because I am with you, and I will help you."

Jeremiah felt unsure at first. He said, "But, Lord, I'm just a young boy. How can I do this?" But God reassured him, "Don't say you're too young. I will give you the words to speak, and I will be with you every step of the way."

Jeremiah had to warn the people that if they didn't turn away from their sinful ways, they would face consequences. But he didn't just say hard things. He also shared the hope God had for them. He told them that God wanted to forgive them and bless them if they would only listen to His words.

Even though the people didn't always listen, Jeremiah didn't give up. He stood strong and did what God told him to do. He trusted that God would take care of him, even when things were tough.

One of the most famous things Jeremiah did was to tell the people about a new covenant—a promise from God. God said, "I will put My law in their hearts. I will forgive their sins, and they will know Me personally. I will be their God, and they will be My people."

Even though Jeremiah's job was difficult, he knew that God's plan was bigger than anything he could see. God's love and promises gave him the strength to keep going.

Jesus's Message to You...

Jeremiah's story teaches you that sometimes, standing up for what's right is hard, but God is with you, and He will help you. Even when people don't listen, you can trust that God's plan is always good. God has a promise for you: He will forgive your sins and help you grow closer to Him.

CHAPTER 25

LAMENTATIONS: GOD'S LOVE IN OUR SADNESS

The prophet Jeremiah wrote a book called Lamentations—a word that means "sad songs" or "tears." Jeremiah wrote this book after the city of Jerusalem was destroyed, and it was a very sad time for the people of Israel. The walls of the city had fallen, and many people had been taken away. It seemed like all hope was lost.

Jeremiah was deeply sad about what had happened to his people and his city. He cried out to God, "How could this happen, Lord? Why did all this sadness come to us?" Jeremiah felt alone and broken-hearted, and he wanted God to hear his cries.

But even though Jeremiah was very sad, he didn't forget about God's love. In the middle of all the tears, he remembered something very important: "The Lord's love never ends! His mercy is new every morning. Great is His faithfulness!"

Even though the people had made bad choices and faced punishment, Jeremiah knew that God's love was still there, and that one day, He would restore His people.

Jeremiah also prayed, "Lord, I will put my hope in You, even though things are hard. You are the one who can help us, and You are always with us, even in our sadness."

Even though Lamentations is a book of tears and sorrow, it's also a reminder that God is faithful and full of mercy. His love is bigger than our pain, and even when we feel sad, we can always turn to Him. Jeremiah's story in Lamentations teaches us that it's okay to feel sad and cry when bad things happen. Even in our sadness, God's love is never far away, and God's mercy and faithfulness are new every day, and He always gives us hope.

Jesus's Message to You...
Lamentations teaches you that My love never stops, even when you're sad. When you feel down, come to Me. I will comfort you and give you new hope every day.

CHAPTER 26

EZEKIEL: GOD'S AMAZING POWER AND PROMISE

There was a prophet named Ezekiel. He lived in a time when the people of Israel were far away from their land and living in a place called Babylon. The Israelites had made many wrong choices, and because of that, they had been taken away from their home.

One day, while Ezekiel was by a river, something amazing happened. He saw a great vision of God's glory! He saw a throne with wheels that sparkled like fire and creatures that had wings and faces like lions, oxen, and eagles. It was a sight so wonderful and powerful that Ezekiel fell on his face in awe.

Then God spoke to him: "Ezekiel, I have chosen you to be a prophet to My people. Tell them that even though they have sinned, I am still with them. I will not leave them, and I have a plan to bring them back."

Ezekiel's job wasn't easy. He had to deliver some hard messages. He warned the people that they needed to turn back to God and stop their sinful ways. He told them that they would face punishment if they didn't change, but he also shared a message of hope.

One of Ezekiel's most famous visions came when God showed him a valley full of dry bones. The bones were scattered everywhere, and they were very dry, which meant they had been dead for a long time.

God asked Ezekiel, "Can these bones live?"

Ezekiel wasn't sure what to say, so he answered, "Only You know, Lord."

God told him to speak to the bones. As Ezekiel did, something incredible happened! The bones started to come together, and muscles and skin appeared on them. Soon, the valley was full of people who were alive again!

God told Ezekiel, "This is what I will do for My people. Though they are scattered and feel like they are dead, I will bring them back to life. I will give them a new heart and a new spirit. I will restore them, and they will be My people, and I will be their God."

Jesus's Message to You...
Ezekiel's story shows that I bring life and hope, even when things seem impossible. I want to give you a new heart, full of My love. So, the next time you feel like you've messed up or are too far from God, remember Ezekiel's vision of the dry bones. God can bring life to anything, and He can bring you back to Him too!

CHAPTER 27

DANIEL: TRUSTING GOD IN THE TOUGHEST TIMES

A long, long time ago, there was a young man named Daniel. He lived in Judah, but one day, the kingdom was taken over by the Babylonians. Daniel and many other young people were taken away to live in the big city of Babylon.

Even though Daniel was far from home, he chose to stay true to God. He prayed to God every day, and he refused to eat food that was not right for him according to God's laws. Daniel knew that no matter where he was, God was always with him.

One day, the king of Babylon, King Nebuchadnezzar, had a strange dream. He didn't understand it, so he called his wise men to help him. But no one could tell him the meaning of the dream. The king was angry and decided to punish them all.

When Daniel heard about this, he prayed to God and asked for help. That night, God showed Daniel the dream and its meaning. Daniel praised God and thanked Him for the answer.

The next day, Daniel went to the king and said, "I know what your dream means, Your Majesty. God has shown me." He told the king about a great statue in his dream, which represented kingdoms that would rise and fall. Daniel explained that God was in control of everything and that His kingdom would last forever.

The king was amazed! He praised God and made Daniel a ruler in the kingdom.

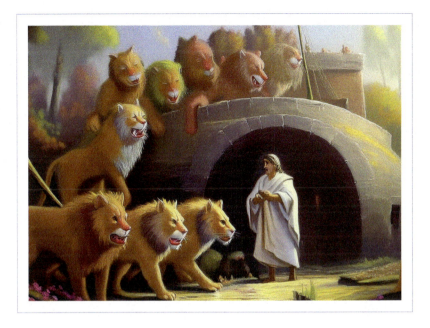

But the story didn't end there. Daniel faced more challenges. One day, the king made a law that everyone had to pray to him. But Daniel refused to stop praying to God. He was thrown into a den of lions as punishment.

But God was with Daniel! He sent an angel to shut the mouths of the lions, and Daniel was safe. The next morning, when the king came to check, Daniel was unharmed! The king was so amazed that he ordered everyone in the kingdom to respect Daniel's God.

Jesus's Message to You…
Daniel's story teaches that no matter where you are, God is always with you, and that you should trust Him, even when things are hard. God has the power to protect you, no matter what happens. Just like Daniel, we can stand strong and trust God, knowing He is with you every step of the way.

HOSEA: GOD'S NEVER-ENDING LOVE

There was a prophet named Hosea. God asked Hosea to do something that seemed very strange: "Hosea, I want you to marry Gomer," God said. Gomer wasn't known for making good choices, but Hosea obeyed God and married her.

At first, things seemed fine. But over time, Gomer made some wrong decisions. She stopped loving Hosea and left him, running after other men. Hosea was heartbroken, but God had a lesson to teach him.

"Go find Gomer," God said. "Bring her back. Show her that you still love her, even though she has been unfaithful."

So, Hosea went to the market, where he found Gomer. She had made bad choices and was now in a terrible situation. Hosea didn't get angry with her. Instead, he lovingly bought her back, telling her, "I still love you, and I want you to be with me."

God told Hosea, "Just like you love Gomer, I love Israel. Even though My people have turned away from Me and made bad choices, I will never stop loving them. I will bring them back, just like you brought Gomer back. My love is faithful, and it never ends."

Hosea's life was a picture of God's love for us. Even when we make mistakes, even when we don't love God like we should, God's love for us never stops. He is always ready to forgive and bring us back to Him.

Jesus's Message to You…
Hosea's message was clear: God's love is faithful. He never stops loving you, even when you make wrong choices, and He wants you to return to Him when you go astray. His love is always there, no matter what. God's love is always ready to welcome you back, just like Hosea welcomed Gomer.

CHAPTER 29

Joel: God Is with Us, Even in Hard Times

There was a prophet named Joel. He lived in a time when the people of Israel were going through a lot of tough situations. A terrible swarm of locusts had come and destroyed all the crops. The fields were empty, and the people were hungry. It was a hard time for everyone.

But even in the midst of this trouble, God had a message for Joel to share. "Tell the people of Israel: return to Me, and I will help you," God said. "Even though things seem bad right now, I am still with you, and I can make everything right again."

Joel shared God's message with the people. "Listen, everyone! God is calling you to turn back to Him. He's ready to forgive you and bless you, but you must change your hearts. Don't just say sorry with your words—show God you mean it by turning away from sin and doing what is right."

Joel also told the people about something wonderful God promised: "In the future, I will pour out My Spirit on everyone—young and old, men and women. You will see dreams and visions, and you will be filled with My love. And anyone who calls on the name of the Lord will be saved."

Joel wanted the people to know that God is full of mercy and love. No matter how bad things get, God is always ready to help us if we turn to Him.

Even though Joel's message started with a warning, it ended with great hope. He reminded the people that God would restore what was lost and bring blessing to those who turn back to Him. God wants us to turn back to Him when we make mistakes, as He is full of mercy and ready to help us, no matter what.

Jesus's Message to You...
Joel's story shows that I am a God of restoration. When you face losses or hard times, trust Me to bring good things into your life. My Spirit will always be with you, guiding and helping you every step of the way.

CHAPTER 30

Amos: God Cares About What's Right

In a little village called Tekoa, there lived a shepherd named Amos. He wasn't a king or a priest, just a regular man who took care of sheep and fig trees. But one day, God called Amos to deliver a very important message. "Amos," God said, "I want you to go to the big cities of Israel and tell the people they are doing wrong."

Amos was surprised. "Me, Lord? I'm just a shepherd!" But Amos obeyed because he loved God and wanted to do what was right.

When Amos arrived in Israel, he saw that things weren't as they should be. The rich people were greedy, taking more than they needed and ignoring the poor. The judges weren't fair, and people were worshiping idols instead of the one true God.

Amos stood in the marketplace and shouted, "Listen to what the Lord says! You think you're doing fine because you're rich and comfortable, but God sees the wrong things you're doing. You are ignoring the poor and the weak. You are cheating people and pretending to love God while your hearts are far from Him."

The people didn't like hearing this. "Who are you to tell us what to do?" they said. But Amos didn't stop. He told them, "God doesn't want fancy songs or big offerings if your hearts are not kind and fair. Let justice flow like a river, and righteousness like a never-ending stream!"

Amos wanted the people to understand that God cares about how we treat others. He doesn't just want us to say we love Him; He wants us to show it by doing what's right.

Even though Amos's message was hard to hear, it was full of love. He reminded the people that God was giving them a chance to change. If they turned back to Him and treated others fairly, He would bless them again. God cares about fairness and justice, and it's not enough to say we love God; we need to show it by how we live.

Jesus's Message to You…
Amos teaches you that I care about justice and kindness. So, the next time you see someone who needs help, or someone being treated unfairly, remember Amos's words: "Let justice flow like a river!"

CHAPTER 31

OBADIAH: A LESSON IN HELPING OTHERS

A long, long time ago, there were two groups of people who didn't get along: the people of Edom and the people of Israel. The Edomites were relatives of the Israelites—both had come from two brothers, Esau and Jacob—but instead of helping Israel when they were in trouble, the Edomites stood by and watched.

One day, God gave a message to a prophet named Obadiah. "Tell the people of Edom that I see what they've done," God said. "You were proud and thought you were safe because you lived high up in the mountains. But you didn't help Israel, your relatives, when they needed you. You even cheered when bad things happened to them. That was wrong."

Obadiah listened carefully and wrote down God's message. "Edom," he said, "you thought you were strong, but God is stronger. You thought you didn't have to care about others, but God sees when you don't help. Your pride and selfishness will be your downfall."

But Obadiah also shared some good news. "One day," he said, "God will make everything right again. He will protect His people, and His kingdom will last forever."

Obadiah's story is short, but it teaches us an important lesson: God cares about how we treat others. So, if we see someone in trouble, God wants us to help. If we see someone hurting, God wants us to show kindness. And if we ever feel proud or think we don't need God, Obadiah reminds us to be humble and trust Him.

The story of Obadiah is like a small but powerful light. It shows us that God wants us to love and help each other because we're all part of His big family.

Jesus's Message to You...
Obadiah shows that I am your defender. Trust Me to bring justice and always choose kindness over revenge. I will take care of you and guide you in love.

CHAPTER 32

Jonah: The Prophet Who Tried to Run Away

Once upon a time, there was a prophet named Jonah. God gave Jonah a very important job: "Go to the big city of Nineveh and tell the people to stop doing wrong. Tell them to turn back to Me."

But Jonah didn't want to go to Nineveh. "Those people are so bad, God," Jonah said. "Why should they get another chance?" So instead of obeying, Jonah decided to run away from God.

He packed his bags and got on a big ship headed in the opposite direction. Jonah thought he could hide from God, but can anyone hide from God? (Hint: Nope!)

As the ship sailed into the sea, a huge storm blew in. The wind howled, and the waves crashed against the ship. The sailors were terrified. "Why is this happening?" they cried. Jonah knew the answer.

"It's my fault," Jonah said. "I'm running away from God. If you throw me into the sea, the storm will stop."

The sailors didn't want to do it, but the storm kept getting worse. Finally, they threw Jonah overboard, and—just as Jonah said—the storm stopped! But Jonah didn't drown. God sent a big fish to swallow him! Inside the belly of the fish, Jonah had lots of time to think. He prayed, "God, I'm sorry for running away. I'll do what You asked me to do."

After three days, the fish spit Jonah out onto dry land. Jonah was slimy and smelly, but he was alive and ready to listen to God.

Jonah went to Nineveh and told the people, "God says to stop doing wrong and turn back to Him, or your city will be destroyed!"

Something amazing happened. The people of Nineveh listened! They were sorry for their sins and prayed to God for forgiveness. And because God is kind and loving, He forgave them.

But Jonah wasn't happy. "God, it's not fair!" Jonah complained. "They were so bad, and You forgave them?"

God gently reminded Jonah, "Shouldn't I care about these people, Jonah? I love them just as much as I love you."

Jonah's story teaches us that God loves everyone, even people who make big mistakes. He wants everyone to turn back to Him and be forgiven. And just like Jonah, we can learn that it's always better to obey God the first time!

Jesus's Message to You...
Jonah's story shows that it's important to listen and obey Me. Even when you make mistakes, I am always ready to forgive you and help you start again. Trust Me, and I will lead you on the right path.

CHAPTER 33

MICAH: WHAT DOES GOD WANT FROM US?

In a small village in Judah, there lived a prophet named Micah. Micah loved God and wanted everyone to know how wonderful He was. But Micah had a tough job—he had to tell the people when they were doing wrong.

The people of Judah were in trouble because they had forgotten God's ways. Some of the leaders were greedy, taking things that didn't belong to them. Others didn't care about the poor or the weak. Instead of worshiping God, many people followed idols made of wood and stone. God sent Micah to tell the people, "Listen up! You're not living the way I taught you. I'm not happy with how you treat others or how you've forgotten Me."

But even as God warned the people, He also gave them hope. Micah said, "God isn't going to leave us. He will send a special Savior, born in Bethlehem, who will lead us back to Him!" The people were surprised. "What does God want from us?" they asked.

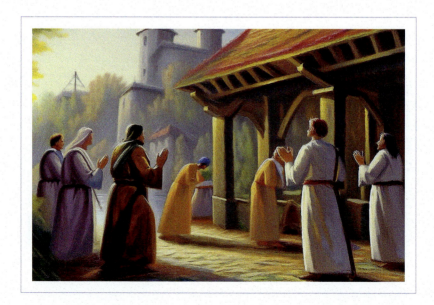

Micah told them, "It's not about fancy gifts or big sacrifices. God wants your hearts. He has shown you what is good: to act justly, to love mercy, and to walk humbly with your God."

What did Micah mean?

- **Act justly:**
  Do what is fair and right. Treat people kindly and stand up for others when they are being treated badly.
- **Love mercy:**
  Be forgiving and kind, just like God is to you. Help others, especially those who need it most.
- **Walk humbly with God:**
  Remember that God is in charge, not us. Talk to Him, trust Him, and follow His ways.

Micah also reminded everyone that God is forgiving. Even though they had done wrong, God was ready to forgive them if they turned back to Him. "God throws our sins into the deepest sea," Micah said. "He remembers them no more!"

The people of Judah learned an important lesson: God isn't impressed by how much we have or how big our offerings are. He cares about how we live, how we treat others, and how much we love Him.

Micah's message wasn't just for the people of Judah; it's for us, too!

Jesus's Message to You…
Micah's words show you how to live for Me. Be kind, love others, and trust Me in everything you do. When you walk with Me, I will fill your life with peace and joy.

CHAPTER 34

Nahum: God Is Strong and Always Right

The prophet Nahum was chosen by God to deliver an important message to a powerful city called Nineveh. You might remember Nineveh as the city where Jonah once went to tell the people to turn back to God. Back then, they listened. But now, many years later, the people of Nineveh were doing bad things again. They were mean to others, especially God's people. They thought they were so powerful that no one could stop them. But God was watching. He always sees what is right and what is wrong.

One day, God spoke to Nahum. "Nahum, I want you to tell the people of Nineveh this: 'I am patient, but I will not let evil go on forever. Your time is up. You have hurt others and turned away from Me, and now you will face the consequences.'"

Nahum knew this was a serious message, so he wrote it down. He told the people, "The Lord is slow to anger and great in power. He is a safe place for those who trust Him, but He will destroy those who keep doing wrong."

God's message was clear: He would protect His people, but Nineveh's time as a strong and powerful city was over.

Nahum also reminded everyone of something very important about God. "The Lord is good," Nahum said. "He is a refuge in times of trouble. He cares for those who trust in Him." This means that God is like a strong castle where you can run and be safe when life feels scary. No matter how big or strong the enemies seem, God is always bigger and stronger.

And just as God said, Nineveh's power came to an end. The city that seemed unstoppable was no match for God's justice.

But for those who loved and trusted God, there was nothing to fear. Nahum's message gave them hope. Even when the world around them felt unfair or scary, they knew God was in control and would take care of them.

Jesus's Message to You...
Nahum's story reminds you that God is patient, but He won't let wrong things last forever. So, whenever life feels unfair or scary, remember Nahum's words: "The Lord is good, a stronghold in the day of trouble. He cares for you!"

CHAPTER 35

HABAKKUK: TRUSTING GOD EVEN WHEN IT'S HARD

In a little village in Judah, there lived a prophet named Habakkuk. He loved God very much and always tried to follow His ways. But Habakkuk had some big, tough questions on his mind.

"God," Habakkuk prayed one evening as the sun set in hues of gold and purple, "why do bad things happen in our land? Why does it seem like the wicked get away with hurting others? I just don't understand."

God listened to Habakkuk's prayer because He always listens when His children talk to Him. And then, in His gentle but powerful voice, God replied: "Habakkuk, I see everything that happens. I know what the wicked are doing, and I will not let their evil go on forever. But for now, I am working out a plan that is bigger than you can see. Trust Me."

This wasn't the answer Habakkuk was expecting. He scratched his head and said, "But God, Your plan is hard to understand. You're going to use an even worse nation to teach us a lesson? That doesn't seem fair!"

God patiently explained again, "Habakkuk, the Babylonians may seem strong now, but their power won't last. I will bring justice in My time. The righteous will live by faith. That means trusting Me even when things don't make sense."

Habakkuk sat quietly for a long moment. He thought about how wise and powerful God is. He thought about how God had always taken care of His people in the past. And then he whispered, "Okay, God. I will trust You."

Then something amazing happened. Habakkuk's heart filled with joy! He realized that no matter how hard life seemed, God was still good, and God was still in control. Habakkuk began to sing a song of praise:

"Even if the fig trees don't grow any fruit,
Even if the fields don't grow any crops,
Even if the sheep are gone from the pen,
I will still be happy because of the Lord!
He is my strength and my joy!"

Habakkuk's song teaches us something very important: We don't always understand God's plans, but we can always trust Him. Just like Habakkuk, we can say, "God, You are good, and I will follow You no matter what!"

Jesus's Message to You…
Habakkuk's story reminds us to look up to God with faith and to keep singing, even when things are hard. Because God is always working, and He always takes care of His children.

CHAPTER 36

ZEPHANIAH: GOD'S LOVE AND JUDGMENT

God gave the prophet Zephaniah an important message to share with the people of Judah. The people were doing many wrong things, worshiping idols, and not following God's commands. Zephaniah's job was to remind them of God's judgment, but also to share the wonderful truth that God still loved them and would give them hope.

Zephaniah started his message by telling the people that God was very sad because they had turned away from Him. He warned them that they would face trouble if they did not change their ways. But Zephaniah didn't just talk about bad things. He also spoke about how God was going to send a special King who would save His people, a King who would bring peace and joy.

Zephaniah's words were hard to hear, but they were also filled with hope. He told the people that even though they had sinned, God would not leave them forever. One day, God would gather His people together, bring them back to their land, and make everything right. God would remove their shame and heal their hearts, bringing joy and singing to those who had been sad.

Zephaniah also reminded the people that God is both loving and just. God loves His people and wants the best for them, but He also must punish sin because He is good and holy. Even though God would bring judgment, He would also bring mercy to those who repent and turn back to Him.

Zephaniah ended his message with a beautiful promise. He said that God would rejoice over His people with singing, that God's love would never fail, and that He would restore what was broken. The people could have joy because God was with them, and He would protect them.

The Book of Zephaniah teaches us that God is both loving and just. He loves us so much that He wants us to live right, but He must punish sin because He is holy. God offers hope, even when we make mistakes.

Jesus's Message to You…
The next time you feel sad or when you see things in the world that aren't right, remember Zephaniah's message. I love you, and I am always ready to forgive and restore you. When you choose to follow Me, you can have joy knowing that I am with you and that I rejoice over you.

CHAPTER 37

HAGGAI: BUILDING GOD'S HOUSE

After God's people returned from being in a faraway land, they had an important job to do: rebuild the temple of God in Jerusalem. But the people became busy with their own houses and forgot about God's house. This made God very sad, and so He sent a prophet named Haggai to remind the people of their special task.

In this book, we learn that God spoke to the people through Haggai, telling them that they needed to rebuild the temple. He reminded them that the temple was the place where God's presence would dwell with them, and it was important to honor God by making it beautiful and holy. But the people had stopped working on the temple because they had focused on their own needs and wanted to make their homes comfortable first.

God was patient with His people, but He wanted them to know that when they obeyed Him and worked together to build the temple, He would bless them. God told them that even though the new temple might not look as glorious as the old one, He would fill it with His glory, and His presence would be there. God reminded them that the temple wasn't just a building—it was a symbol of His love, His faithfulness, and His plan to be with His people.

Haggai encouraged the people to trust God's promises and put God first in their lives. God would help them finish the temple, and He would give them strength and courage to complete the work. The people listened to Haggai's message and started rebuilding the temple with joy and determination.

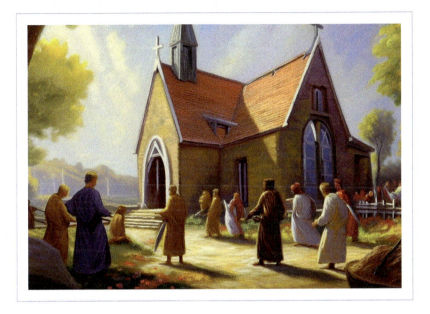

God also gave the people a special promise through Haggai: He would bless them, fill them with His Spirit, and make them strong. He told them that in the future, He would bring peace and prosperity to their land. The people had to trust in God and His timing, knowing that He would keep His promises.

The Book of Haggai teaches us that just like the people of Israel needed to rebuild God's house, we should put God first in our hearts and lives as well. That even when we face challenges, God will be with us and help us, just like He helped the people rebuild the temple.

Jesus's Message to You…
Put Me first in your life. When you focus on loving and serving Me, I will bless you and guide you. Remember, your heart is like a temple where My Spirit lives.

CHAPTER 38

ZECHARIAH: A VISION OF HOPE

God's people had returned from a faraway land to rebuild Jerusalem. But they were still facing many struggles, and their hearts were heavy. In this time of trouble, God sent a prophet named Zechariah to encourage them. Zechariah brought a message of hope, showing the people that God had wonderful plans for them, and that one day, He would send a special Savior.

Zechariah's story begins with visions, or dreams, that God gave him. In these visions, Zechariah saw amazing things! He saw angels, and he saw the work that God was doing behind the scenes, preparing a beautiful future for His people. Some of the visions were a little mysterious, but each one was a reminder that God was in control and that His promises would come true.

One of the most important visions Zechariah saw was of a man called the "Branch." This was a special person who would come from the family of King David. This "Branch" was a picture of the Messiah, Jesus, who would come to save His people. Zechariah also saw that God would clean the hearts of His people, take away their sin, and make them pure again. He would give them new hearts that loved Him.

Zechariah's message wasn't just about the future; it was also about the present. He told the people to not give up, even when things were hard. He reminded them that God was with them and would help them rebuild the temple. When they worked together and trusted in God, they would see His blessings.

Zechariah also gave a beautiful picture of the day when God's kingdom would come. He told the people that there would be a time of peace and joy when God would rule over His people, and everyone would worship Him. God would protect them, and His people would live in safety and happiness.

God's message through Zechariah was clear: He was going to send a Savior to bring peace, and His promises were sure and would come true. Zechariah encouraged the people to keep working and trusting, knowing that God had a plan to bring about His wonderful future.

The Book of Zechariah teaches us that just like Zechariah's visions of the Messiah, God has a beautiful future in store for those who trust in Him. Even when things are hard, God is working behind the scenes and will help us. We can trust that everything God says will happen, and He will keep His word.

Jesus's Message to You...
Zechariah's words were about Me. I am your King who came to bring you salvation. Trust My Spirit to guide and help you, for I love you and have amazing plans for your life. Just like God sent a Savior to Zechariah's people, He has sent Me to save you and bring peace to your heart.

MALACHI: A CALL TO RETURN TO GOD

After God's people had rebuilt their city and the temple, they began to forget about God's love and His commands. The people of Israel were no longer giving God the best of what they had. They were being lazy in their worship, offering sacrifices that weren't the best, and forgetting the promises God had made to them. So, God sent a prophet named Malachi to remind them of His love, to warn them about their actions, and to call them to return to Him.

In the Book of Malachi, God spoke to His people with strong words, telling them that they had not been honoring Him as they should. God wanted them to bring their best offerings, to love and serve Him with all their hearts, and to trust in His plans for the future. The people were confused. They asked God, "Why should we do all this? What have we done wrong?" But God showed them that their hearts were far from Him, and they needed to repent and return to the true worship of God.

Malachi also reminded the people of God's love. Even though they had turned away from God, He still loved them. God spoke of how He had chosen them and made a covenant with them. God's love was unchanging, and He wanted His people to come back to Him, to love Him, and to serve Him faithfully.

One of the most important messages Malachi gave was about a coming messenger. Malachi told the people that God was going to send someone who would prepare the way for the Savior. This messenger would point people to God and tell them about the One who would bring forgiveness and healing. Malachi's message was like a promise: God would send a Savior to rescue His people, and this Savior would come in God's perfect timing.

Finally, Malachi gave the people a reminder of how God had been faithful throughout history. He reminded them of God's justice, that God would punish evil and reward those who lived for Him. Malachi encouraged the people to remember the law of Moses, to live with hope, and to look forward to the day when the Savior would come.

Jesus's Message to You…
Children, Malachi's story shows you that My love for you never changes. I came to be your Savior, bringing you light and healing. Give your heart fully to Me, for you are My treasured child. You can trust that I love you and that I am faithful to keep My promises.

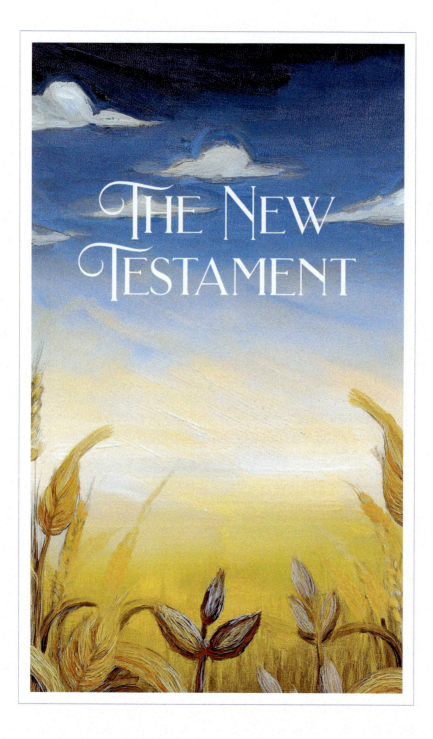

The New Testament

CHAPTER 40

MATTHEW: THE STORY OF JESUS, OUR SAVIOR

Matthew, a follower of Jesus, decided to write a book about Jesus's life to help people understand who Jesus was and why He came to earth. This book is called the Gospel of Matthew. It is the first book in the New Testament of the Bible and tells the story of how Jesus came to save us all.

The Book of Matthew begins with the story of Jesus's birth. Jesus wasn't just any baby—He was the Son of God! His mother, Mary, was a young woman who was chosen by God to be His mother. Mary's husband, Joseph, was a good man who trusted God, even when he didn't fully understand what was happening. One night, an angel appeared to Joseph in a dream and told him that Mary would have a baby who was the Savior of the world. This baby would be called Jesus, which means "the Lord saves."

When Jesus was born, a star appeared in the sky, and wise men from far away followed the star to find Him. They brought gifts for the baby Jesus: gold, frankincense, and myrrh. The shepherds, who were taking care of their sheep, also heard about Jesus's birth and came to see Him. They were amazed and praised God for sending His Son into the world.

As Jesus grew up, He began to teach people about God's kingdom. He taught them that God loves everyone and that they should love one another. He performed many miracles, like healing the sick, giving sight to the blind, and even raising the dead. People followed Jesus because they could see that He was special and that He had the power to do amazing things.

One day, Jesus gathered a group of disciples—people who would follow Him and learn from Him. He taught them about love, forgiveness, and how to live in a way that pleased God. Jesus told His disciples to love their enemies, to pray for those who hurt them, and to trust God with all their hearts. He said that God's kingdom wasn't about being the most powerful or the most important but about serving others and putting others first.

As Jesus continued His ministry, He faced opposition from the religious leaders, who didn't like the way He was teaching. But Jesus didn't stop. He knew that He had a mission to fulfill—to save the world from sin. One day, Jesus went to Jerusalem, where He was arrested and sentenced to die on a cross. But the story didn't end there. Three days later, Jesus rose from the dead! His resurrection showed that He was truly the Son of God and that He had power over death.

Before Jesus went back to heaven, He gave His disciples a mission: to go and make disciples of all nations. He told them to baptize people and teach them to obey everything He had commanded. Jesus promised to be with them always, even until the end of the world.

The Book of Matthew teaches us that Jesus came to save us from our sins and bring us into a relationship with God. He showed us that we should love one another, forgive our enemies, and put others first. Through His death and resurrection, Jesus has overcome sin and death, offering us eternal life with God. As His followers, we are called to share His love with others and make disciples of all nations.

Jesus's Message to You…
The next time you hear My story, remember that I am your Savior, and that I love you more than you can imagine. I want you to follow Me, love others, and share My good news with the world.

CHAPTER 41

MARK: THE AMAZING ADVENTURES OF JESUS

There was a man named Mark who wanted to tell everyone about Jesus. Mark's book is called the Gospel of Mark, and it's full of exciting stories about the amazing things Jesus did while He was on earth.

The story of Mark's Gospel begins with John the Baptist, who came to prepare the way for Jesus. John told people to repent and be baptized, for the Savior was coming! One day, Jesus came to John to be baptized, and when He came up out of the water, the heavens opened, and the Holy Spirit descended like a dove. A voice from heaven said, "This is My Son, whom I love; with Him, I am well pleased." This was the beginning of Jesus's ministry.

Jesus didn't waste any time. He began to travel from town to town, telling people about the kingdom of God and performing miracles. He healed the sick, made blind people see, and even calmed a storm with just a word. People were amazed at the things He did, and they began to follow Him wherever He went.

One of the most exciting parts of the Book of Mark is when Jesus calls His disciples. Jesus picked twelve men to be His closest friends and followers. They left everything behind—their jobs, their families, and their homes—to follow Jesus. They watched Jesus perform miracles, and they learned from Him every day.

But Jesus didn't just perform miracles for fun—He did them to show people that He was the Son of God and that He had the power to heal, forgive, and save. One of the most incredible miracles Mark tells us about is when Jesus raised a little girl from the dead. He told her, "Little girl, I say to you, get up!" And she did! Jesus showed everyone that He had power over life and death.

Jesus also taught people about the love of God. He told them stories, called parables, to help them understand how much God loved them and wanted them to follow Him. Jesus taught that the greatest commandment was to love God with all your heart and to love your neighbor as yourself. He also told His followers to be servants, to put others first, and to forgive those who wronged them.

But not everyone was happy with what Jesus was teaching. The religious leaders didn't like how Jesus was changing things, and they became jealous of Him. Eventually, they arrested Jesus and took Him to trial. They accused Him of doing wrong, and even though He had never sinned, they sentenced Him to die on a cross.

Jesus died on the cross for our sins, but that wasn't the end of the story. Three days later, Jesus rose from the dead! His disciples were amazed, and Jesus showed them that He had truly conquered death. He appeared to them and gave them one last command: "Go into all the world and preach the good news to all creation."

The Book of Mark teaches us that Jesus has the power to heal, forgive, and give eternal life. He showed us how to love and serve others, even when it's hard. Through His death and resurrection, Jesus offers forgiveness and eternal life to all who believe in Him. Just like Jesus told His disciples, we are also called to share the good news with others.

Jesus's Message to You...
Always remember how much I love you and how much I want you to follow Me. I gave My life for you, so that you can live forever with Me. Follow Me with all your heart!

CHAPTER 42

LUKE: IT'S A WONDERFUL LIFE

Like the books by Matthew and Mark, Luke decided to write down everything he had learned about Jesus. Luke's book is called the Gospel of Luke, and it tells the amazing story of Jesus's life, from His birth to His resurrection, in a way that is easy to understand and full of love.

The story of Luke's Gospel begins with the birth of Jesus. A young woman named Mary, who was engaged to a man named Joseph, was visited by an angel. The angel told Mary that she was going to have a baby, and that this baby would be the Son of God! Mary was surprised, but she trusted God's plan. Mary and Joseph traveled to Bethlehem, where Jesus was born in a humble stable because there was no room for them in the inn. A bright star shone in the sky, and angels sang to the shepherds, telling them about the birth of the Savior.

When Jesus was just a little boy, His parents took Him to the temple in Jerusalem. There, an old man named Simeon, and a prophetess named Anna both recognized that Jesus was the promised Savior, and they praised God for sending Him into the world.

As Jesus grew up, He began to teach the people about God's love. He told them that God's kingdom was open to everyone, even the poor and the outcasts. Jesus didn't just teach with words; He showed God's love by healing the sick, giving sight to the blind, and casting out demons. He even brought dead people back to life! People were amazed by His power, but what they loved most was how kind and loving He was.

One of the things that Luke focuses on is how Jesus loved everyone, especially those whom others didn't care about. Jesus showed love to tax collectors, sinners, and those who were forgotten by society. He told stories, called parables, to teach people about God's kingdom. One of His most famous stories is about the Good Samaritan—a story of a man who helped a stranger in need, showing that love for others should have no limits.

Jesus also taught His disciples how to pray. He taught them the Lord's Prayer, which begins with, "Our Father in heaven, hallowed be Your name." Jesus showed them that God is a loving Father who listens to their prayers and wants to help them.

But as Jesus's popularity grew, not everyone was happy with what He was doing. The religious leaders didn't like that He was changing things, so they began to plot against Him. Jesus knew what was coming, and He bravely continued His mission.

One of the most powerful moments in Luke's Gospel is when Jesus shared a special meal with His disciples before He died. He took bread and wine, saying that they represented His body and blood, which would be broken and poured out for the forgiveness of sins. Jesus knew that He was going to die on the cross, but He wanted His disciples to remember Him through this meal.

After Jesus died on the cross, His followers were heartbroken. But on the third day, something amazing happened—Jesus rose from the dead! He appeared to His disciples, showing them that He was alive and had conquered death. Before He went back to heaven, He told His disciples to go into all the world and tell others about the good news of His resurrection.

The Book of Luke teaches us that Jesus showed kindness to the poor, sinners, and outcasts, teaching us to love all people. He came to bring God's kingdom to earth, to heal the sick, forgive sins, and offer eternal life through His death and resurrection. Not only did Jesus teach us to pray and trust God to meet our needs, but He asked us all to tell others about the good news of Jesus, just like His disciples did.

Jesus's Message to You...
Little ones, remember that I love you, I came to earth to save you, and I want you to follow Me with all your heart. Just like My disciples, I want you to share My story with others and live with the hope of eternal life.

CHAPTER 43

John: The Great Love of Jesus

John, who was one of Jesus's closest friends, wrote a special book called the Gospel of John, which tells us about Jesus in a very deep and loving way. John wanted everyone to know that Jesus is not just a man, but the Son of God, sent to show us how much God loves us.

The Book of John begins by telling us something amazing: Jesus is not just a baby born in Bethlehem—He is the eternal Word of God, who was with God from the very beginning of time. John wrote, "In the beginning was the Word, and the Word was with God, and the Word was God." This means that Jesus has always existed, and He was with God before the world was made. Jesus created everything, and He came to the world to show us God's love.

John points out that when Jesus came to earth, He became a human being, just like us. He was born as a baby, grew up, and lived a perfect life. Jesus didn't just talk about love—He showed love. He healed the sick, helped the poor, and comforted those who were sad. Jesus even turned water into wine at a wedding to help a couple in need, showing His care for the little things in life.

One of the most famous stories in John's book is about a man named Nicodemus. Nicodemus was a religious leader who came to Jesus at night, wanting to understand more about God. Jesus told him that to see God's kingdom, he needed to be "born again." This means that we must have a new heart, one that believes in Jesus and trusts Him as our Savior.

John also tells us about one of the most beautiful verses in the Bible: "For God so loved the world that He gave His one and only Son, that whoever believes in Him shall not perish but have eternal life." This verse tells us that God loves us so much that He sent Jesus to die for our sins so that we can be with Him forever. Jesus didn't come to judge us; He came to save us!

As Jesus continued His ministry, He performed many miracles that showed His power and love. He healed blind people, fed thousands of people with just a few loaves of bread and fish, and even raised people from the dead! One of the most powerful miracles John tells us about is when Jesus raised His friend Lazarus from the dead. Jesus called Lazarus out of his tomb, and Lazarus came back to life! This miracle showed that Jesus has power over death, and that He is the resurrection and the life.

Not everyone believed in Jesus, however. The religious leaders were jealous of Him and didn't like the way He was teaching. They decided to arrest Jesus and have Him crucified. Jesus knew this was part of God's plan, and He was willing to die for the sins of the world. He was beaten, and He carried a cross to the hill where He would be crucified. On the cross, Jesus said, "It is finished," and He gave His life for us.

But the story didn't end there. Three days later, Jesus rose from the dead! His disciples were filled with joy and amazement. Jesus appeared to them and showed them His scars, proving that He had truly come back to life. Before He went back to heaven, He told His disciples to love one another and to tell others about Him. He promised that He would send the Holy Spirit to help them.

The Book of John teaches us that Jesus has always existed, and that He came to earth to show us God's love. So much so, Jesus came to die for our sins and offer us eternal life with God. He is the resurrection and the life, and He offers us hope beyond the grave. Just as Jesus loves us, we are to love others and share the good news about Him.

Jesus's Message to You…
I want you to know that I came to earth to save you, and I want you to follow Me with all your heart. Yes, I am the Son of God, the Savior of the world, and I promise to be with you always.

CHAPTER 44

Acts: The Adventures of the Early Church

After Jesus rose from the dead and went back to heaven, His disciples were left to carry on His mission. The Book of Acts, written by Luke, tells us all about the amazing adventures the disciples had as they spread the good news of Jesus. It's a story full of courage, miracles, and the power of the Holy Spirit.

After Jesus went back to heaven, His disciples were gathered when something amazing happened. The Holy Spirit came down upon them, like a mighty wind and tongues of fire. The Holy Spirit filled them with power, and they began to speak in different languages. This was a sign that the good news of Jesus was for everyone, no matter where they came from. Peter, one of Jesus's disciples, stood up and began to preach to the crowds, telling them about Jesus. That day, three thousand people became followers of Jesus!

As the disciples traveled from city to city, they performed many miracles in Jesus's name. They healed the sick, cast out demons, and even raised people from the dead. But they didn't do it alone—the Holy Spirit was with them, giving them strength and helping them spread God's love. The disciples knew that they had a special job: to tell everyone about Jesus and to make more disciples.

One of the most exciting parts of Acts is the story of Saul, a man who hated Christians and was trying to stop the spread of the gospel. But one day, as Saul was on his way to a city called Damascus, a bright light suddenly blinded him. It was Jesus! Jesus asked Saul, "Saul, Saul, why are you persecuting Me?" Saul realized that Jesus was real and that he had been wrong. Jesus told Saul to go to Damascus, where he would meet a Christian named Ananias who would help him. Saul's eyes were healed, and he became one of the greatest leaders of the early church, changing his name to Paul.

Paul traveled all over the world, telling people about Jesus, starting churches, and encouraging believers. He faced many dangers along the way—being arrested, beaten, and even shipwrecked! But no matter what happened, Paul never gave up. He knew that God was with him, and he trusted God's plan.

The Book of Acts also tells us about the first Christians and how they loved each other and cared for one another. They shared everything they had and prayed together every day. They were a big family, and they loved God and loved each other.

But not everyone was happy with what the disciples were doing. The religious leaders often tried to stop them, and some of them were even thrown in jail! But the disciples didn't let fear stop them. They boldly continued to tell people about Jesus, knowing that the message of God's love had to be shared with everyone.

In the final chapters of Acts, we see Paul going to Rome to stand trial. Even though he was in prison, Paul continued to tell people about Jesus. He was a faithful servant of God, and he knew that God was using him in powerful ways, even in difficult times. The Book of Acts ends with Paul preaching in Rome, sharing the good news of Jesus, and showing that nothing can stop the message of God's love.

The Book of Acts teaches us that just like the disciples, we have the Holy Spirit to guide us and give us strength. The disciples didn't keep the good news to themselves—they told everyone about Jesus, and we are called to do the same. Even someone like Saul, who hated Christians, was changed by Jesus and became one of the greatest missionaries of all time.

Jesus's Message to You…
Just like the early Christians, I call you to love and care for one another. Remember how the disciples trusted in God and spread His love to the world? I ask you to be part of that mission too! You can share the good news and love others, just like the early Christians did.

CHAPTER 45

ROMANS: THE LETTER OF GOD'S AMAZING GRACE

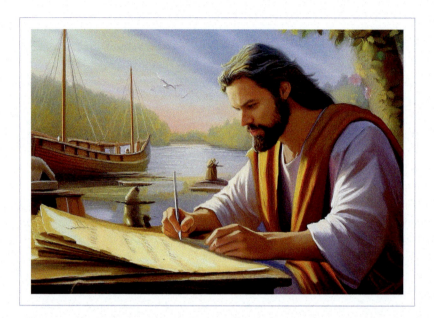

The apostle Paul wrote a letter to the believers in Rome. This letter is called the Book of Romans, and it is one of the most important letters in the Bible. In it, Paul explains God's amazing love, how Jesus came to save us, and how we should live as His followers. The Book of Romans is full of big ideas, but it's also filled with hope and grace.

The book begins with a big truth: all people, no matter who they are, have sinned.

Sin is anything we do that goes against God's perfect ways. It can be telling lies, being unkind, or thinking bad thoughts. Paul explains that we all fall short of God's glory, and no one is perfect. But there is good news! Even though we've all made mistakes, God loves us, and He has a plan to save us.

Paul says that the way we are saved is through faith in Jesus Christ.

Jesus came to the earth, lived a perfect life, and died on the cross for our sins. When Jesus died, He took the punishment for our sins so that we could be forgiven. But the story didn't end there—Jesus rose from the dead, showing that He has the power over sin and death! Through Jesus, we can be made right with God, not because we are good enough, but because of His grace and love.

One of the most important messages in Romans is about grace. Grace means that God gives us His love and forgiveness as a free gift. We don't have to earn it or work for it; it's something that God freely gives to us because He loves us so much. Paul writes that salvation is not about following rules or doing good things—it's about trusting in Jesus and accepting His gift of grace.

Paul also explains that when we trust in Jesus, we are made new. We are no longer slaves to sin, but we become children of God. This means that we have a new identity in Christ! We are part of God's family, and we have the Holy Spirit living inside us to help us live the way God wants us to live.

Paul encourages believers to live in a way that pleases God. He says that we should love one another, be kind and patient, and forgive each other just as God has forgiven us. Paul tells us that we should use the gifts God has given us to serve others and build up the church. God has a special plan for each of us, and He wants us to live with purpose, sharing His love with the world.

In Romans, Paul also talks about how God has a plan for Israel and the world. Even though many of the Jewish people didn't believe in Jesus, God is not done with them. He has a plan to bring them back to Him, and everyone who believes in Jesus, whether Jew or Gentile, is part of God's family. Paul encourages all believers to trust in God's timing and plan.

The Book of Romans teaches us that we've all made mistakes and need God's forgiveness and that we can't earn God's love, but He freely gives it to us through Jesus Christ. He died for our sins and rose again, so we can have eternal life with Him. When we trust in Jesus, we are given a new identity as God's children. So, as believers, we are called to serve others, love one another, and share God's grace with the world. His plan is bigger than we can understand, and we can trust that He will work everything out according to His will.

Jesus's Message to You…
The next time you read the Book of Romans, remember that My Father loves you so much. He has given you the gift of salvation through Me, Jesus, and He wants you to live a life full of love, grace, and purpose. You are part of My family, and I have a great plan for your life!

CHAPTER 46

1 Corinthians: Living for Jesus

The apostle Paul wrote a letter to the believers in a city called Corinth. This letter, called 1 Corinthians, was filled with wisdom and guidance because the Corinthians were facing many challenges. Paul wanted to remind them how to live for Jesus and love one another as part of God's family.

The Corinthians had some disagreements and arguments. They were choosing sides, saying, "I follow Paul," or "I follow Apollos." Paul told them that this wasn't the way to act. He said, "Is Christ divided?" and reminded them that Jesus is the one they should follow. Paul explained that Jesus is the foundation of their faith, and everything they do should be built on Him.

Paul talked about God's wisdom, which is different from the wisdom of the world. He said that the message of the cross might seem foolish to some people, but to those who believe, it is the power of God. Paul reminded the Corinthians that God chose what seems weak to the world to show His strength. This means that God doesn't look for the smartest or most powerful people—He works through those who trust in Him.

The Corinthians also had questions about how to live as followers of Jesus. Paul gave them advice about many things, like how to live in peace with others, how to love their families, and how to use the gifts God gives them to help the church. He explained that each person has special gifts from God, like teaching, helping, or encouraging, and that all these gifts are important for building up God's family.

One of the most beautiful parts of Paul's letter is when he talks about love. He says that love is the greatest gift of all. Paul describes love this way: "Love is patient, love is kind. It does not envy, it does not boast, it is not proud. It does not dishonor others, it is not self-seeking, it is not easily angered, it keeps no record of wrongs." Paul wanted the Corinthians to know that no matter how gifted or smart they were, without love, it didn't mean much.

Paul also reminded the Corinthians about the Lord's Supper, a special way to remember Jesus's sacrifice.

He explained that when believers eat the bread and drink the cup, they are remembering that Jesus gave His body and blood to save them. Paul told them to treat this time with respect and to remember Jesus with thankful hearts.

At the end of the letter, Paul talks about the resurrection of Jesus and the hope it brings to all believers. He explained that because Jesus rose from the dead, everyone who believes in Him will also be raised to live with God forever. Paul says, "Death has been swallowed up in victory. Where, O death, is your victory? Where, O death, is your sting?" This means that Jesus has defeated death, and those who trust in Him don't need to be afraid.

Paul encouraged the Corinthians to stand firm in their faith and to keep working for God. He reminded them, "Always give yourselves fully to the work of the Lord, because you know that your labor in the Lord is not in vain."

Jesus's Message to You…
Love one another, just as I love you. Remember, the greatest thing you can do is to live in love. Trust in Me, and I will give you hope, strength, and a heart full of joy.

CHAPTER 47

2 Corinthians: God's Power in Weakness

The apostle Paul wrote a second letter to the believers in Corinth. This letter, called 2 Corinthians, was written to encourage them, remind them of God's promises, and teach them about the power of God's grace in every part of life.

Paul started by praising God for being the "Father of compassion and the God of all comfort." He told the Corinthians that God comforts us in our troubles so that we can comfort others. When we face hard times, God is always there to help us, and He uses those experiences to make us better at helping others.

Paul shared with the Corinthians about the difficulties he had faced as he traveled to tell people about Jesus. He said that sometimes he felt so weak and overwhelmed that he didn't know what to do. But Paul trusted in God's strength, not his own. He explained that when we trust in God, He will deliver us from our troubles and give us the strength to keep going.

Paul reminded the Corinthians about the importance of forgiveness. He told them about someone in their church who had done something wrong and encouraged them to forgive that person. Paul said that when we forgive others, we show the love of Jesus, who has forgiven us.

One of the most beautiful parts of this letter is when Paul talks about God's glory. He said that when we believe in Jesus, God changes us to be more like Him. Paul explained that this change happens because of the Holy Spirit, who lives in us. He said, "And we all, who with unveiled faces contemplate the Lord's glory, are being transformed into His image with ever-increasing glory."

Paul also talked about how fragile we are, like clay jars. He said, "But we have this treasure in jars of clay to show that this all-surpassing power is from God and not from us." This means that even though we might feel weak or ordinary, God's amazing power shines through us.

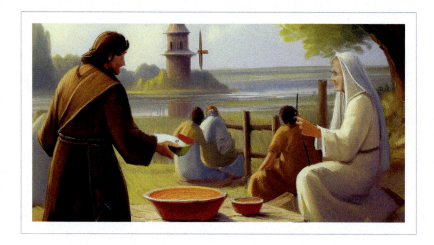

Paul wanted the Corinthians to know that they could always rely on God's grace. He shared something personal: he had a problem, which he called a "thorn in the flesh," and he had prayed for God to take it away. But God told him, "My grace is sufficient for you, for My power is made perfect in weakness." Paul learned that even when he felt weak, God's power would give him strength. He said, "When I am weak, then I am strong."

Paul also reminded the Corinthians about generosity. He encouraged them to give to help others in need. He said, "God loves a cheerful giver," and reminded them that when we give, God will always provide for us.

At the end of the letter, Paul reminded the Corinthians that they should keep focusing on Jesus and living in peace with one another. He told them to encourage each other and to remember that God's love and grace are always with them.

Jesus's Message to You...
I want you to know that My grace is enough for you. Even when you feel weak, I am strong for you. Trust Me, and I will help you through everything. Let My love fill your heart so you can share it with others.

CHAPTER 48

GALATIANS: THE FREEDOM OF GRACE

The apostle Paul wrote a letter to the believers in Galatia. This letter, called Galatians, was full of passion and urgency because Paul wanted the Galatians to understand something very important: Jesus has set us free! Paul had heard that some people were teaching the Galatians that they needed to follow certain rules and laws to be right with God, but Paul wanted to remind them that Jesus has already done everything we need to be saved.

At the beginning of the letter, Paul explains that the good news (the gospel) is that Jesus Christ came to save us from our sins. No one can be saved by following rules or being good enough—salvation comes only through trusting in Jesus and His death on the cross for our sins. Paul says, "Grace and peace to you from God our Father and the Lord Jesus Christ, who gave Himself for our sins to rescue us from the present evil age." This means that Jesus gave His life to rescue us from the power of sin and to bring us into a relationship with God.

Paul warns the Galatians that they should not be fooled by anyone who teaches that they need to follow other things, like the old laws from the Jewish Bible, to be saved. He reminds them that the gospel of Jesus is all they need. When we try to add anything to Jesus's work, it's like saying His sacrifice wasn't enough, and that is not true. Jesus alone is enough to save us.

In Galatians, Paul talks a lot about grace—the free gift of God's love and forgiveness. Grace means that we don't have to earn God's love by doing good works; instead, He gives it to us because He loves us. Paul says that if we try to earn God's love by following rules, then we are no longer relying on God's grace. But God's grace is what truly saves us, and it's what makes us right with Him.

Paul explains that God's grace is a gift that brings freedom. Jesus sets us free from the burden of trying to follow every rule perfectly, and we can live in the freedom of knowing that Jesus has done it all for us. "It is for freedom that Christ has set us free," Paul writes. When we believe in Jesus, we are no longer slaves to sin or to the law—we are free!

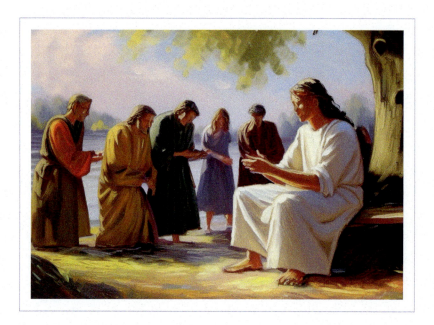

Now that the Galatians knew they were free in Christ, Paul wanted them to understand how they should live as people who are free. He told them that living by the Spirit was the key. When we trust in Jesus, God gives us the Holy Spirit to help us live the way He wants us to live. The Holy Spirit helps us show love, joy, peace, patience, kindness, goodness, faithfulness, gentleness, and self-control. These are called the fruit of the Spirit, and they are the things that should be growing in our lives as we follow Jesus.

Paul also reminds the Galatians that, although they are free, they should not use their freedom to hurt others or to sin. Instead, they should love others and serve one another. "You, my brothers and sisters, were called to be free. But do not use your freedom to indulge the flesh; rather, serve one another humbly in love."

Paul wanted the Galatians to understand that following Jesus is about faith, not works. He uses the story of Abraham to explain this. Abraham was a man in the Old Testament who trusted in God, and that faith made him right with God. It wasn't because Abraham followed all the laws perfectly—it was because he trusted in God. Paul says, "So those who rely on faith are blessed along with Abraham, the man of faith."

In the end, Paul encourages the Galatians to keep walking in the freedom they have in Christ. He tells them to remember that their salvation is a gift, and they should not go back to trying to follow a bunch of rules to be saved. Jesus did it all for them, and that's enough.

Jesus's Message to You…
I give you My love and forgiveness as a free gift. When you trust in Me, the Holy Spirit will help you with love, joy, peace and all the fruit of the Spirit.

CHAPTER 49

EPHESIANS: THE GIFT OF UNITY AND LOVE

The apostle Paul wrote a letter to the believers in a city called Ephesus. This letter, called Ephesians, was written to help them understand the amazing blessings they had in Jesus and to encourage them to live in unity and love. Paul wanted them to know how much God loved them and how they could live as part of God's family.

At the beginning of his letter, Paul reminds the Ephesians of the incredible gifts God has given them. He says that before the world was made, God chose them to be His children through Jesus. Isn't that amazing? Paul writes, "He chose us in Him before the creation of the world to be holy and blameless in His sight." This means that God's love for us is not something we have to earn—it's a gift He planned from the very beginning.

Paul explains that Jesus's death on the cross brings us forgiveness for our sins and makes us part of God's family. Through Jesus, we are adopted as God's children! This means that no matter who we are or where we come from, we belong to God's family when we trust in Jesus.

Paul also talks about the power of God's Spirit living inside us. When we believe in Jesus, God gives us the Holy Spirit as a seal or promise. This is like God saying, "You are Mine, and I will never leave you." The Holy Spirit helps us grow closer to God and live the way He wants us to.

One of the most important parts of Ephesians is when Paul talks about unity. He reminds the Ephesians that Jesus came to bring people together. In those days, there were many groups of people who didn't get along, like Jews and Gentiles. But Paul explains that Jesus breaks down all the walls that divide us. "For He Himself is our peace, who has made the two groups one and has destroyed the barrier, the dividing wall of hostility." Through Jesus, we can all be part of one big family—God's family! Paul encourages the Ephesians to live in a way that shows they are God's children. He tells them to be kind, forgiving, and loving. "Be completely humble and gentle; be patient, bearing with one another in love." He also reminds them that God has given each of us special gifts to serve others and to help the church grow.

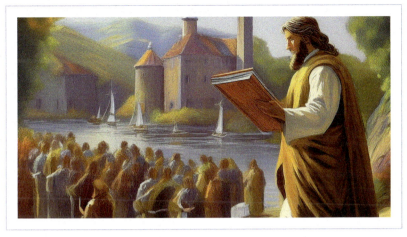

Another big theme in Ephesians is love. Paul says that God's love for us is so big, we can't even fully understand it! He prays that the Ephesians will know how wide, long, high, and deep the love of Jesus is. Paul wants them to feel so loved by God that they can't help but love others.

Paul also gives advice about how to live as followers of Jesus in everyday life. He talks about being kind to our families, obeying our parents, and treating others with respect. He reminds them to shine God's light in the world by doing what is good and right.

At the end of his letter, Paul gives a special picture to help the Ephesians understand how to stay strong in their faith. He tells them to put on the "armor of God." This armor includes things like the belt of truth, the breastplate of righteousness, and the shield of faith. It's like wearing God's protection so we can stand strong against anything that tries to pull us away from Him.

Jesus's Message to You...
You are never alone because My Spirit is with you, helping you to live with kindness and love. Remember, I give you strength, and I bring you peace. Trust in Me and let My love shine through you!

CHAPTER 50

Philippians: The Joy of Knowing Jesus

The apostle Paul wrote a letter to the believers in Philippi. This letter, called Philippians, is full of encouragement and joy. Even though Paul was in prison when he wrote it, his heart was happy because he loved Jesus so much. Paul wanted the Philippians to know that no matter what happens in life, we can always find joy in knowing Jesus.

At the beginning of his letter, Paul thanks the Philippians for their friendship and support. He tells them how much he prays for them and how thankful he is that they are sharing the good news of Jesus with others. "I thank my God every time I remember you," Paul writes. He reminds them that God, who started His good work in their lives, will carry it on until it is finished. This means that God will never stop helping us grow in faith!

One of the most important messages in Philippians is about joy. Paul tells the Philippians to rejoice in the Lord always! But how could Paul feel joyful while he was in prison? It's because his joy didn't depend on his circumstances—it came from knowing Jesus. Paul says, "I can do all things through Christ who gives me strength." Jesus gives us strength and joy, no matter what we face.

Paul also encourages the Philippians to live in a way that shows they belong to Jesus. He tells them to think about others and not just themselves. "Do nothing out of selfish ambition or vain conceit. Rather, in humility, value others above yourselves." He reminds them that Jesus is the perfect example of humility. Even though Jesus is God, He came to earth as a servant and gave His life for us.

Paul writes about the power of knowing Jesus. He says that nothing in the world is more important than having a relationship with Him. Paul says, "I consider everything a loss because of the surpassing worth of knowing Christ Jesus my Lord." This means that all the things we think are important—like achievements or possessions— are nothing compared to the joy of knowing Jesus.

Paul also encourages the Philippians to keep growing in their faith and not give up. He says, "Forgetting what is behind and straining toward what is ahead, I press on toward the goal to win the prize for which God has called me heavenward in Christ Jesus." Paul compares life to a race, and the prize is spending forever with Jesus.

Another key message in Philippians is about peace. Paul tells the Philippians not to worry about anything but to pray about everything. He says, "The peace of God, which transcends all understanding, will guard your hearts and your minds in Christ Jesus." This means that when we trust God with our worries, He fills our hearts with a peace that is bigger than anything we can imagine.

Finally, Paul reminds the Philippians to think about good things. "Whatever is true, whatever is noble, whatever is right, whatever is pure, whatever is lovely, whatever is admirable—if anything is excellent or praiseworthy—think about such things." When we fill our minds with good and godly thoughts, we stay close to Jesus and experience His joy.

Jesus's Message to You...
Be full of joy because I am always with you. No matter what happens, you can trust Me to give you strength. When you feel worried, tell Me about it in prayer, and I will fill your heart with peace. Keep your eyes on Me, and I will help you run the race of life with joy and love!

CHAPTER 51

Colossians: Jesus Is All We Need

The apostle Paul wrote a letter to the believers in a city called Colossae. This letter, called Colossians, was written to help them understand something very important: Jesus is the greatest, and He is all we need. Paul wanted to remind them that Jesus is above everything and that knowing Him changes how we live.

At the beginning of the letter, Paul tells the Colossians how thankful he is for their faith and love. He prays that they will grow in their knowledge of God and live in a way that pleases Him. Paul writes, "We continually ask God to fill you with the knowledge of His will through all the wisdom and understanding that the Spirit gives." He wants them to know God better and to live strong and joyful lives for Jesus.

One of the most important messages in Colossians is about who Jesus is. Paul says that Jesus is the image of the invisible God. This means that when we look at Jesus, we see what God is like! He also says that Jesus created everything in heaven and on earth and that all things hold together because of Him. Isn't that amazing? Jesus isn't just a teacher or a helper—He is God, and He oversees everything!

Paul explains that Jesus came to rescue us from sin and bring us back to God. Through His death on the cross, Jesus made a way for us to be forgiven and become part of God's family. Paul says, "For God was pleased to have all His fullness dwell in Him, and through Him to reconcile to Himself all things." Because of Jesus, we can be friends with God and live in His love.

Paul also warns the Colossians not to be tricked by false teachings. Some people were telling the Colossians that they needed to follow special rules or do certain things to be close to God. But Paul reminds them that Jesus is enough. "In Christ, all the fullness of the Deity lives in bodily form, and in Christ you have been brought to fullness." This means that when we have Jesus, we don't need anything else to make us right with God.

Paul encourages the Colossians to live like people who belong to Jesus. He says that because Jesus has given us new life, we should set our hearts and minds on things above, not on earthly things. This means we should focus on loving God and others, not just on getting more stuff or doing things for ourselves.

Paul gives the Colossians some practical advice about how to live for Jesus. He tells them to get rid of things like anger, lying, and selfishness and to instead clothe themselves with kindness, humility, gentleness, and patience. He says, "And over all these virtues put on love, which binds them all together in perfect unity." Love is the most important thing because it shows that we belong to Jesus.

Paul also reminds them to let the peace of Christ rule in their hearts and to be thankful. He says, "Whatever you do, whether in word or deed, do it all in the name of the Lord Jesus, giving thanks to God the Father through Him." This means that everything we do—whether it's helping a friend, obeying our parents, or praying—should be done for Jesus.

At the end of his letter, Paul encourages the Colossians to keep praying and sharing the good news about Jesus with others. He reminds them that Jesus is the greatest treasure, and He is worth sharing with everyone!

Jesus's Message to You...
Know that I am above all things, and I love you more than you can imagine. You don't need to do anything special to be close to Me—I am always with you. Trust in Me, and let My love guide your heart. Remember, I will help you live with kindness, love, and joy every day!

CHAPTER 52

1 Thessalonians: Encouragement for God's Family

The apostle Paul wrote a letter to the believers in Thessalonica. This letter, called 1 Thessalonians, was filled with love and encouragement because Paul cared deeply for them. He wanted to remind them to keep growing in their faith and to stay strong, even when life was hard.

Paul began by thanking God for the Thessalonians. He told them that their faith, love, and hope were shining examples for others to see. Paul said, "You became a model to all the believers." The way they trusted in Jesus and shared His love was like a bright light that encouraged people in other cities to follow Jesus too.

Paul reminded the Thessalonians how they first heard the good news about Jesus. He told them that the gospel came to them "not simply with words but also with power, with the Holy Spirit and deep conviction." This means that when they heard about Jesus, the Holy Spirit helped them believe and trust in Him completely.

Paul talked about the importance of living in a way that pleases God. He encouraged the Thessalonians to keep growing in holiness and love. Paul reminded them, "It is God's will that you should be sanctified." "Sanctified" means becoming more like Jesus every day by loving God and obeying His Word.

One of Paul's most important messages was about love. He said, "Now about your love for one another . . . you do love all of God's family throughout Macedonia. Yet we urge you, brothers and sisters, to do so more and more." Paul wanted the Thessalonians to keep loving others, showing kindness, and helping those in need.

Paul also gave the Thessalonians hope about what happens when Jesus comes back. He explained that Jesus will return one day, and when He does, everyone who believes in Him will be with Him forever. Paul said, "The Lord Himself will come down from heaven, with a loud command, with the voice of the archangel and with the trumpet call of God." He told them not to be sad about people who had died in Christ because they would rise again and be with Jesus too.

Paul encouraged the Thessalonians to live as children of the light. He explained that believers are not in the dark because they know about Jesus. Paul said, "You are all children of the light and children of the day. We do not belong to the night or to the darkness." He reminded them to stay awake, be ready, and live in faith, hope, and love as they wait for Jesus's return.

At the end of the letter, Paul shared simple but powerful advice:
- "Rejoice always."
- "Pray continually."
- "Give thanks in all circumstances."

These words remind us to keep our hearts focused on God no matter what is happening.

Paul closed his letter by reminding the Thessalonians that God is faithful. He said, "The one who calls you is faithful, and He will do it." This means that God will always keep His promises and help us live for Him.

Jesus's Message to You…
I see your faith, your love, and your hope in Me, and it makes My heart glad. Keep growing in love and shining as lights for others. Remember, I will come back for you, and you will be with Me forever. Trust in My promises and live each day with joy and hope.

CHAPTER 53

2 Thessalonians: Faith and Hope

The apostle Paul wrote a second letter to the believers in Thessalonica. This letter, called 2 Thessalonians, was written to encourage them to stay strong in their faith, remind them of God's justice, and give them hope about Jesus's return.

Paul began by thanking God for the Thessalonians. He told them how proud he was of their growing faith and love for one another. Even though they were facing hard times and persecution, they didn't give up. Paul said, "We boast about your perseverance and faith in all the persecutions and trials you are enduring."

Paul reminded the Thessalonians that God sees everything. He told them that one day, God would make everything right. People who had been cruel to them would face God's justice, and those who believed in Jesus would be rewarded with rest and joy in God's presence. Paul said, "God is just: He will pay back trouble to those who trouble you and give relief to you who are troubled."

Paul also wanted to clear up confusion about Jesus's return. Some people were saying that Jesus had already come back, and this made the Thessalonians worried. Paul explained that certain things had to happen before Jesus returned, including the rise of someone Paul called the "man of lawlessness," who would try to lead people away from God. But Paul assured them that Jesus would defeat this evil one with His power and glory when He came back.

Paul reminded the Thessalonians not to be afraid or shaken. He said, "Stand firm and hold fast to the teachings we passed on to you." Paul wanted them to trust in what they had learned about Jesus and the gospel, knowing that God had chosen them to be saved through their faith in Jesus.

Paul encouraged the Thessalonians to pray and to trust in God's strength. He said, "May the Lord direct your hearts into God's love and Christ's perseverance." This meant that even in tough times, they could rely on God's love to guide them and Jesus's example of perseverance to keep going.

Paul also talked about working hard and being responsible. He noticed that some people had stopped working because they thought Jesus was coming back soon. Paul reminded them that while they waited for Jesus, they needed to live faithfully and take care of their responsibilities. He said, "The one who is unwilling to work shall not eat."

At the end of the letter, Paul prayed that God would give the Thessalonians peace and strength. He said, "May the Lord of peace Himself give you peace at all times and in every way. The Lord be with all of you."

Jesus's Message to You…
I see when you are scared or tired, and I want you to know that I am always with you. Don't be afraid. Keep trusting in Me, and I will give you the strength you need. Stand firm in My love and share it with others while you wait for My return.

CHAPTER 54

1 Timothy: A Guide for God's People

The apostle Paul wrote a letter to a young man named Timothy. Timothy was like a spiritual son to Paul and a faithful leader in the church. Paul wanted to help Timothy understand how to guide the believers in their faith and how the church should work. This letter, called 1 Timothy, is full of wisdom about living for Jesus and being part of God's family.

At the start of the letter, Paul tells Timothy to stay in the city of Ephesus and make sure people were teaching the truth about God. Some people had started spreading wrong ideas, and Paul wanted Timothy to remind everyone about the good news of Jesus. Paul says that God's plan is for people to know Him through faith in Jesus, not through made-up stories or arguments.

Paul talks a lot about the gospel—the good news that Jesus Christ came to save sinners. He even says, "Here is a trustworthy saying that deserves full acceptance: Christ Jesus came into the world to save sinners—of whom I am the worst." Paul wanted Timothy to know that God's grace is big enough for everyone, no matter how much they've messed up.

Paul also explains how believers should live. He tells Timothy that prayer is very important, and that people should pray for everyone, including their leaders. He says, "God wants all people to be saved and to come to a knowledge of the truth." When we pray, we trust that God can work in the lives of others.

In his letter, Paul talks about how the church should be organized. He tells Timothy to choose leaders who love Jesus and live in a way that honors God. These leaders, called elders and deacons, should be wise, kind, and full of faith. Paul says that the church is like a family, and every person in God's family is important.

Paul also warns Timothy about people who will try to lead others away from the truth. He says that Timothy should teach the truth with love and courage. Paul reminds him, "Don't let anyone look down on you because you are young, but set an example for the believers in speech, in conduct, in love, in faith, and in purity." Even though Timothy was young, God had given him the strength to be a leader.

Throughout the letter, Paul tells Timothy to focus on what really matters: loving God and loving others. He says that some people will care more about money or arguments than about following Jesus, but Timothy should stay faithful. Paul writes, "But godliness with contentment is great gain." This means that knowing God and trusting Him is the best treasure of all.

At the end of the letter, Paul encourages Timothy to keep fighting the good fight of faith. He says, "Take hold of the eternal life to which you were called." Paul wants Timothy to remember that his hope is in Jesus, and Jesus will help him stay strong no matter what.

Jesus's Message to You…
I have called you to be part of My family. Pray, love others, and follow the truth. I will help you be strong and faithful, just like Timothy. Trust in Me, and I will guide you every step of the way.

CHAPTER 55

2 Timothy: Finishing Strong

The apostle Paul wrote a second letter to his dear friend and spiritual son, Timothy. This letter is called 2 Timothy, and it's a very special letter because it's the last one Paul wrote before he went to be with Jesus. Paul knew his time on earth was almost over, so he wanted to share important words of encouragement and wisdom with Timothy.

Paul begins by reminding Timothy of his faith. He says, "I am reminded of your sincere faith, which first lived in your grandmother, Lois and in your mother, Eunice and, I am persuaded, now lives in you also." Paul wanted Timothy to remember the strong faith passed down to him and to hold on to it no matter what.

Paul encourages Timothy to be brave and bold for Jesus. He says, "For the Spirit God gave us does not make us timid, but gives us power, love, and self-discipline." Paul knows that Timothy might face hard times for sharing the good news of Jesus, but he reminds him that God's Spirit will give him all the strength he needs.

In the letter, Paul talks about the hard times Christians will face. He says some people will turn away from the truth and do what is wrong. But Paul tells Timothy, "Preach the word; be prepared in season and out of season; correct, rebuke, and encourage—with great patience and careful instruction." Paul wants Timothy to keep teaching others about Jesus, even when it's hard.

Paul also tells Timothy to guard the truth of the gospel. He says, "What you heard from me, keep as the pattern of sound teaching, with faith and love in Christ Jesus. Guard the good deposit that was entrusted to you—guard it with the help of the Holy Spirit who lives in us." Paul knew the gospel was the most important message, and he wanted Timothy to protect it and pass it on.

One of the most famous parts of 2 Timothy is when Paul talks about the Bible. He says, "All Scripture is God-breathed and is useful for teaching, rebuking, correcting, and training in righteousness, so that the servant of God may be thoroughly equipped for every good work." Paul wanted Timothy to know that God's Word is powerful and will help him and others grow in their faith.

Paul shares about his own life, too. He says, "I have fought the good fight, I have finished the race, I have kept the faith." Paul is saying that he stayed faithful to Jesus all the way to the end of his life, and he knows he will receive a reward from Jesus in heaven. He wants Timothy to stay faithful, too, no matter how hard it gets.

At the end of the letter, Paul gives Timothy personal instructions and asks him to come visit soon. Even though Paul is in prison, he knows he is never alone because Jesus is always with him. He says, "The Lord will rescue me from every evil attack and will bring me safely to His heavenly kingdom." Paul trusts Jesus completely, and he wants Timothy to trust Him too.

Jesus's Message to You...
Be brave and hold on to your faith. My Spirit is with you, giving you power, love, and self-discipline. Read My Word and share it with others. Finish strong, just like Paul, and remember that I am always with you. Keep your eyes on Me, and I will guide you safely home.

CHAPTER 56

Titus: Honoring God

The apostle Paul wrote a letter to his friend Titus, who was a leader in the church on the island of Crete. Paul wanted to help Titus understand how to guide the believers and teach them to live in a way that honors God. This letter, called Titus, is full of advice on how Christians should live, work together, and show God's love to others.

Paul starts by reminding Titus about the truth of the gospel. He says that God, who never lies, promised long ago to bring eternal life through Jesus Christ. Paul wants Titus to teach the believers that their hope is found in Jesus, who gave Himself to save us from our sins.

One of the first things Paul tells Titus is to choose wise and godly leaders for the church. These leaders, called elders, should be people who love God and live in a way that reflects His goodness. Paul says elders should not be quick to get angry, greedy, or selfish, but instead, they should love what is good and teach others about Jesus.

Paul also gives Titus advice on how all believers should live. He says older men should be wise and self-controlled, older women should teach younger women to love their families, younger men should be respectful and self-controlled, and servants should work hard and be honest. Paul wants everyone in the church to live in a way that shows the beauty of God's teachings.

Paul reminds Titus that God's grace teaches us how to live. He says, "For the grace of God has appeared that offers salvation to all people. It teaches us to say no to ungodliness and worldly passions, and to live self-controlled, upright, and godly lives in this present age." Paul wants the believers to know that God's grace not only saves us but also helps us live in a way that pleases Him.

Paul talks about the importance of doing good works. He says, "Our people must learn to devote themselves to doing what is good, in order to provide for urgent needs and not live unproductive lives." These good works are not what saves us, but they show others that God's love is at work in us.

Paul also warns Titus about people who cause trouble by arguing or teaching things that are not true. He says Titus should stay focused on teaching what is true and helpful, not getting caught up in useless arguments. Paul tells Titus to remind the believers to be kind, gentle, and ready to do good to everyone.

At the end of the letter, Paul encourages Titus to keep teaching the believers to live in a way that honors God. He says that Christians should remember how much God has done for them. "He saved us, not because of righteous things we had done, but because of His mercy." Paul wants everyone to know that salvation is a gift from God, and we should live lives full of gratitude and love because of it.

Jesus's Message to You...
I saved you because I love you, not because of anything you could do. My grace is a gift, and it will help you live a life that honors Me. Be kind, do good to others, and let your actions show My love. Keep your eyes on Me, and I will guide you every day.

CHAPTER 57

PHILEMON: FORGIVENESS AND LOVE

The apostle Paul wrote a short but heartfelt letter to a man named
Philemon. Philemon was a Christian and a leader in the church who
had a servant named Onesimus. Onesimus had run away from
Philemon, but something amazing happened—he met Paul and
became a believer in Jesus!

Paul writes this letter to Philemon to ask him to forgive Onesimus
and welcome him back, not just as a servant, but as a brother in
Christ. This letter, called Philemon, is a beautiful picture of forgiveness,
love, and how Jesus changes relationships.

Paul starts by telling Philemon how thankful he is for him. He says,
"I always thank my God as I remember you in my prayers, because
I hear about your love for all His holy people and your faith in the
Lord Jesus." Paul wants Philemon to know that his love for others has
been an encouragement to many.

Then, Paul shares why he is writing. He tells Philemon about Onesimus, who has become like a son to Paul during his time in prison. Paul explains that Onesimus is now a follower of Jesus, and that changes everything. "Formerly he was useless to you, but now he has become useful both to you and to me." Paul is making a play on words here because the name "Onesimus" means "useful."

Paul gently asks Philemon to forgive Onesimus and welcome him back. He says, "I am sending him—who is my very heart—back to you. Perhaps the reason he was separated from you for a little while was that you might have him back forever—no longer as a slave, but better than a slave, as a dear brother." Paul wants Philemon to see Onesimus not just as a servant but as a fellow believer and part of God's family.

Paul even offers to make things right if Onesimus owes Philemon anything. He says, "If he has done you any wrong or owes you anything, charge it to me. I, Paul, am writing this with my own hand. I will pay it back." This shows how much Paul cares about both Philemon and Onesimus, and it reminds us of how Jesus paid the price for our sins so we could be forgiven.

At the end of the letter, Paul expresses his confidence in Philemon. He says, "Confident of your obedience, I write to you, knowing that you will do even more than I ask." Paul believes Philemon will not only forgive Onesimus but go above and beyond in showing love and grace to him.

Even though this letter is very short, it teaches us a lot about forgiveness and how Jesus brings people together. Because of Jesus, we are part of one big family, and we should love and forgive each other, just as God has forgiven us.

Jesus's Message to You...
I have forgiven you because I love you so much. When someone hurts you or does something wrong, remember how much I have forgiven you and show that same forgiveness to others. Love each other as brothers and sisters in My family, and let My grace bring you together.

CHAPTER 58

HEBREWS: DON'T GIVE UP

The letter called Hebrews was written to encourage believers who were going through hard times. These Christians were tempted to give up and go back to their old ways of worshiping God under the law. But the writer of Hebrews wanted them to know something very important: Jesus is better than anything or anyone else, and He is all we need to be close to God.

The letter begins by reminding the readers that God has spoken to His people in many ways throughout history—through prophets, angels, and the Scriptures. But now, God has spoken to us through His Son, Jesus. Jesus is the exact representation of God's being, and He holds everything together by His powerful Word.

The writer explains that Jesus is greater than the angels because He is the Son of God. He is also greater than Moses, who led God's people out of slavery in Egypt. While Moses was a faithful servant in God's house, Jesus is the builder of the house and the Son who rules over it.

The letter spends a lot of time talking about how Jesus is our great High Priest. In the Old Testament, the high priests had to offer sacrifices again and again for the sins of the people. But Jesus offered Himself as the perfect sacrifice once and for all. Because of His death and resurrection, we can be forgiven and have a close relationship with God.

One of the most beautiful verses in Hebrews says, "Let us then approach God's throne of grace with confidence, so that we may receive mercy and find grace to help us in our time of need." This means that because of Jesus, we can come to God anytime, and He will welcome us with love and kindness.

The writer also talks about faith. In chapter 11, sometimes called the "Hall of Faith," we learn about people like Noah, Abraham, Sarah, Moses, and many others who trusted God even when they couldn't see how everything would work out. These people weren't perfect, but they believed that God would keep His promises, and He did.

Hebrews encourages believers to keep their eyes on Jesus, especially when life gets hard. The writer says, "Let us run with perseverance the race marked out for us, fixing our eyes on Jesus, the pioneer and perfecter of faith." Jesus went through suffering and even died on the cross, but He didn't give up. Now, He is seated at the right hand of God, and He helps us keep going when we feel like giving up.

The letter also reminds us to live in a way that pleases God. We are called to love others, help those in need, and worship God with thankful hearts. Hebrews says, "Through Jesus, therefore, let us continually offer to God a sacrifice of praise—the fruit of lips that openly profess His name."

The message of Hebrews is clear: Jesus is better. He is better than the old laws, better than the sacrifices, and better than anything else we could ever rely on. Because of Jesus, we have hope, forgiveness, and the promise of eternal life.

Jesus's Message to You...
I am all you need. When life is hard, keep your eyes on Me. I love you so much that I gave My life for you so that you can always be close to God. Trust Me, and I will help you every step of the way. Remember, I will never leave you or let you down!

CHAPTER 59

JAMES: LIVING OUT YOUR FAITH

James wrote a letter to Christians to help them live out their faith in everyday life. James was the brother of Jesus, and he became a leader in the church after Jesus went back to heaven. In his letter, James talks about how true faith in Jesus should show in the way we live, the choices we make, and how we treat others.

James begins by encouraging believers to stay strong when life is hard. He says, "Consider it pure joy, my brothers and sisters, whenever you face trials of many kinds." Why would James say that? Because challenges help us grow stronger in our faith! When we trust God during hard times, He helps us become more patient and mature.

One of the most important messages in James is that faith isn't just about what we believe—it's also about what we do. James says, "Faith by itself, if it is not accompanied by action, is dead." That means if we really believe in Jesus, our actions will show it. For example, if we see someone in need, we should help them, not just say nice words. James reminds us that faith and good deeds go hand in hand.

James also talks about the power of words. He says that our tongues are small but very powerful—like a tiny spark that can start a big fire. He warns us to be careful with our words because they can either build people up or tear them down. James encourages us to use our words to bless others and not to hurt them.

Another lesson in James is about treating everyone with kindness and fairness. He warns against showing favoritism, like giving special attention to rich people while ignoring the poor. James reminds us that God loves everyone the same, and we should too. He says, "Love your neighbor as yourself," and treat others the way Jesus would.

James also talks about wisdom. He says there are two kinds of wisdom—worldly wisdom and heavenly wisdom. Worldly wisdom can make people selfish and proud, but heavenly wisdom comes from God and is full of peace, kindness, and humility. James says, "If any of you lacks wisdom, you should ask God, who gives generously to all without finding fault, and it will be given to you."

Finally, James reminds us to trust God in everything. He says we should pray when we're in trouble, sing songs of praise when we're happy, and pray for others who are sick or in need. James says, "The prayer of a righteous person is powerful and effective." God listens to our prayers, and He is always ready to help us.

The letter of James is like a guidebook for living a life that honors Jesus. It reminds us that our faith should make a difference in how we live, speak, and love others. When we follow Jesus, people will see His love in everything we do!

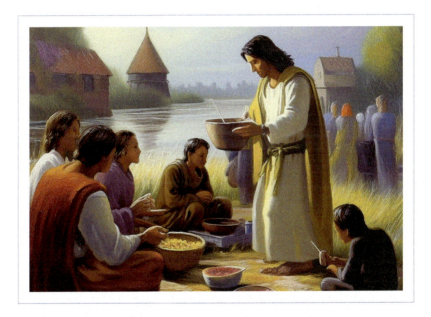

Jesus's Message to You...
I want your faith to grow big and strong, like a tree that bears good fruit. Trust Me, and I will help you live in a way that shows My love to others. Remember to be kind, to help those in need, and to use your words to bring joy and peace.

CHAPTER 60

1 Peter: Hope in Hard Times

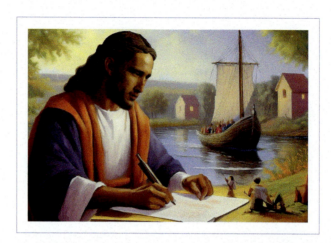

The apostle Peter wrote a letter to Christians who were going through really tough times. These believers were being mistreated because of their faith in Jesus, and they needed encouragement to stay strong. Peter wanted them to know that no matter how hard life got, they could have hope because of what Jesus had done for them.

Peter begins his letter by reminding the believers that they are God's chosen people. He says, "Praise be to the God and Father of our Lord Jesus Christ! In His great mercy, He has given us new birth into a living hope through the resurrection of Jesus Christ from the dead." This living hope means that, because Jesus rose from the dead, we can be sure that we will live forever with Him.

Peter encourages the believers to rejoice, even in their suffering, because hard times help their faith grow stronger. He compares their faith to gold, which is tested and purified by fire. Just like fire makes gold shine brighter, trials make our faith stronger and more beautiful in God's eyes.

One of Peter's big messages is about how Christians should live in a world that doesn't always understand them. He calls them to be holy, which means to live in a way that pleases God. Peter reminds them that they are like strangers or travelers in this world because their real home is in heaven.

Peter also talks about how special God's people are. He says, "You are a chosen people, a royal priesthood, a holy nation, God's special possession, that you may declare the praises of Him who called you out of darkness into His wonderful light." This means that every believer has an important role in showing God's love to the world.

Peter gives practical advice about how to live as followers of Jesus. He tells the believers to respect others, even those who treat them unfairly. He encourages them to follow Jesus's example, who suffered without complaining or fighting back. Peter says, "When they hurled their insults at Him, He did not retaliate; when He suffered, He made no threats. Instead, He entrusted Himself to Him who judges justly."

Peter also reminds the believers to love one another deeply. He says, "Above all, love each other deeply, because love covers over a multitude of sins." This means that when we love others, we forgive them and help them see God's love through us.

Another big message in Peter's letter is about standing firm in faith when facing spiritual battles. He warns believers that the devil is like a roaring lion looking for someone to devour. But Peter encourages them to resist the devil by staying strong in their faith and trusting in God.

In the end, Peter reminds us that their suffering won't last forever. He says, "And the God of all grace, who called you to His eternal glory in Christ, after you have suffered a little while, will Himself restore you and make you strong, firm, and steadfast." God promises to help His children and bring them to a place of peace and joy with Him forever.

Jesus's Message to You...
I see you, and I know when life feels hard. When you feel scared or sad, trust in Me, because I will help you stand strong. You are so special to Me, and I have a wonderful home waiting for you in heaven.

CHAPTER 61

2 Peter: Growing in Grace and Standing Firm

The apostle Peter wrote a second letter to Christians to remind them of important truths about following Jesus. He knew his time on earth was almost over, and he wanted to encourage believers to grow strong in their faith, stay on guard against false teachers, and look forward to the day when Jesus would come back.

Peter begins his letter by reminding Christians of the amazing promises God has given them. He says, "His divine power has given us everything we need for a godly life through our knowledge of Him who called us by His own glory and goodness." This means that God gives us all the strength and wisdom we need to live in a way that pleases Him.

Peter encourages believers to grow in their faith by adding things like goodness, knowledge, self-control, perseverance, godliness, kindness, and love to their lives. He says, "If you possess these qualities in increasing measure, they will keep you from being ineffective and unproductive in your knowledge of our Lord Jesus Christ." Peter wants Christians to keep growing and becoming more like Jesus every day.

One of Peter's main messages is to remind Christians of the truth they already know. He says, "I will always remind you of these things, even though you know them and are firmly established in the truth you now have." Peter doesn't want anyone to forget the good news of Jesus or the way they should live because of it.

Peter also warns believers to watch out for false teachers. These are people who say things that sound good but are not true. They try to lead people away from Jesus. Peter says false teachers are like wells without water—they promise something good but don't deliver. He tells Christians to stay focused on God's Word and not be tricked by things that go against the Bible.

In the letter, Peter talks about how God has everything under control, even when it seems like the world is a mess. Some people were saying that Jesus wasn't coming back, but Peter reminds believers that God is patient because He wants everyone to have a chance to repent and be saved. Peter says, "The Lord is not slow in keeping His promise, as some understand slowness. Instead, He is patient with you, not wanting anyone to perish, but everyone to come to repentance."

Peter explains that Jesus will come back like a thief in the night—unexpectedly. He tells believers to be ready by living holy and godly lives. He says, "But in keeping with His promise we are looking forward to a new heaven and a new earth, where righteousness dwells." This is a beautiful reminder that God will make everything new and perfect one day.

Peter finishes his letter by encouraging Christians to grow in their faith and trust in God's grace. He says, "Grow in the grace and knowledge of our Lord and Savior Jesus Christ. To Him be glory both now and forever!" Peter wants every believer to stay close to Jesus and keep growing in their relationship with Him.

Jesus's Message to You...
I want you to keep growing strong in Me, like a tree with deep roots that stands tall in any storm. Remember My promises, and don't be afraid of false ideas—My Word is always true. I am coming back one day to make everything new and perfect. Keep trusting Me, and let My love grow in your heart every day. I love you, and I am with you always!

CHAPTER 62

1 JOHN: LIVING IN GOD'S LOVE

The apostle John wrote a letter to Christians to help them understand what it means to live in God's love. John wanted believers to know the truth about Jesus, to love one another, and to walk in the light of God's truth. This letter, called 1 John, is all about how we can have a close relationship with God and with each other.

John starts his letter by reminding us of the amazing truth about Jesus. He says, "That which was from the beginning, which we have heard, which we have seen with our eyes, which we have looked at and our hands have touched—this we proclaim concerning the Word of life." John is talking about Jesus, who came to earth to show us who God is. Jesus wasn't just a man; He is the Son of God, and through Him, we can have eternal life.

One of John's big messages is that God is light. He says, "God is light; in Him there is no darkness at all." This means that God is pure and holy, and there is no sin in Him. John tells us that if we want to have a close relationship with God, we need to walk in His light by living in a way that pleases Him.

But what happens when we mess up? John has good news! He says, "If we confess our sins, He is faithful and just and will forgive us our sins and purify us from all unrighteousness." God loves us so much that He forgives us when we admit our sins and turn back to Him.

John also talks a lot about love. He says, "Dear friends, let us love one another, for love comes from God. Everyone who loves has been born of God and knows God." John explains that God is love, and if we truly know Him, His love will show in the way we treat others.

John reminds us of the greatest act of love: "This is how we know what love is: Jesus Christ laid down His life for us." Because Jesus gave His life for us, we should be willing to show love and kindness to others, even when it's hard.

Another big part of John's letter is about truth. John warns us to be careful about false teachers who don't believe the truth about Jesus. He says, "Whoever denies that Jesus is the Christ does not have the Father." John wants us to stay strong in our faith and always trust in the truth of God's Word.

John also gives us a beautiful promise: "See what great love the Father has lavished on us, that we should be called children of God! And that is what we are!" When we believe in Jesus, we become part of God's family forever.

John finishes his letter by reminding believers to stay close to God. He says, "Dear children, keep yourselves from idols." This means we should love God more than anything else in the world. When we put God first, we can live in His love and share it with others.

Jesus's Message to You...
I want you to walk in My light and stay close to Me. When you make mistakes, don't worry—I will forgive you when you turn to Me. Love one another, just as I have loved you. Remember, you are My precious child, and I am always with you!

CHAPTER 63

2 John: Walking in Truth and Love

The apostle John wrote a short letter to a Christian woman and her children. In this letter, he wanted to remind them of two very important things: to live in truth and to love one another. John knew that these two things were key to living a life that pleases God.

John begins the letter by calling the woman and her children "chosen by God" and saying that he loves them in the truth. He reminds them that love for God means obeying His commands. He says, "And this is love: that we walk in obedience to His commands." To love God is to follow His ways, just like Jesus showed us by obeying God perfectly.

John also talks about the truth and how important it is to love one another. He encourages them to keep showing love by living the way God has taught us. Jesus came to earth, lived a perfect life, and gave Himself for our sins. That's the truth we should hold on to and live by. When we live in that truth, we honor God and share His love with others.

One of John's big concerns in this letter is about false teachers. He warns the lady and her children to be careful of anyone who does not bring the true message of Jesus. John says, "If anyone comes to you and does not bring this teaching, do not take them into your house or welcome them." John wants them to protect themselves and their families from anyone who tries to teach something that is not true about Jesus.

Even though John is warning them about false teachers, he reminds them that they should still love others. Love means speaking the truth in kindness, and John wants them to show love to everyone while staying true to God's Word. He says, "I have much to write to you, but I do not want to use paper and ink. Instead, I hope to visit you and talk with you face to face, so that our joy may be complete."

John ends his letter by sending greetings from other believers who are with him. He encourages them to keep walking in truth and love and reminds them that both are important in following Jesus.

Jesus's Message to You…
Be careful of anyone who teaches things that are not true about Me. Stay close to the truth, and your joy will be full. I love you, and I'm always with you, guiding you in love and truth!

CHAPTER 64

3 John: Hospitality and Living in Truth

The apostle John wrote a short letter to his friend Gaius. In this letter, John encouraged Gaius to continue living in the truth, showing love, and helping others, especially those who were spreading the message of Jesus. John's letter is a beautiful reminder of how we can serve God by caring for one another and walking in His truth.

John begins by expressing his love for Gaius. He says, "Dear friend, I pray that you may enjoy good health and that all may go well with you, even as your soul is getting along well." John is happy to hear that Gaius is walking in the truth, living in a way that pleases God. He says, "I have no greater joy than to hear that my children are walking in the truth." For John, seeing people live in the truth of God's Word brings him great joy.

John then talks about the importance of showing hospitality, especially to those who are spreading the gospel. He praises Gaius for being kind to these traveling teachers of the Word, saying, "It was good of you to provide for them in this way and send them on their way in a manner worthy of God." John reminds Gaius that by helping those who are serving God, he is also serving God Himself.

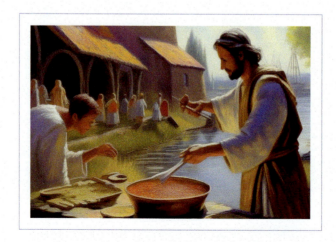

In the letter, John also talks about a man named Diotrephes. Diotrephes was a leader in the church who did not welcome others and even rejected the teachings of John. He wanted to be first and was causing trouble in the church. John warns Gaius not to follow the bad example of Diotrephes. Instead, John encourages him to follow the good example of others who live in the truth and show kindness. He says, "Dear friend, do not imitate what is evil but what is good."

Finally, John shares his hope that he will be able to visit Gaius soon. He ends the letter by telling Gaius that he has been a good example to others and encouraging him to continue walking in the truth. John says, "Peace to you. The friends here send their greetings. Greet the friends there by name."

Jesus's Message to You...
Just like Gaius helped those who were spreading the good news, you can help others and show kindness. When you do good things for others, you are serving Me. Remember to always follow good examples and keep walking in the truth. I love you, and I'm with you as you serve and love others!

CHAPTER 65

JUDE: STAYING STRONG IN THE FAITH

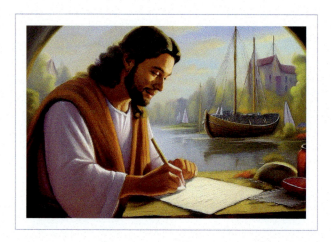

A man named Jude wrote a letter to encourage Christians to stand strong in their faith and to be careful about people who would try to lead them away from God. Jude's letter is a reminder of the importance of holding onto the truth of God's Word and staying true to what we believe in Jesus.

Jude begins by saying that he is writing to those who are loved by God and called to be His followers. He tells them, "Mercy, peace, and love be yours in abundance." Jude's heart is full of care for these believers, and he wants them to stay strong in the faith.

Jude explains that he had originally planned to write a letter about salvation and the good things God has done for us, but he felt led to write about something more urgent. He wanted to warn them about false teachers who were secretly trying to change the message of Jesus. Jude says, "For certain individuals whose condemnation was written about long ago have secretly slipped in among you." These false teachers were spreading lies and trying to lead people away from God's truth.

Jude reminds them that these people are not following God's way and are causing trouble in the church. He warns them that these false teachers are selfish, arrogant, and causing division. But Jude encourages the believers not to be discouraged. He reminds them of God's judgment against those who live in sin, pointing to stories from the Old Testament, like the angels who rebelled and the people of Israel who didn't trust God. Jude tells them, "Woe to them! They have taken the way of Cain."

Despite the danger of these false teachers, Jude encourages the believers to remain faithful. He says, "But you, dear friends, by building yourselves up in your most holy faith and praying in the Holy Spirit, keep yourselves in God's love as you wait for the mercy of our Lord Jesus Christ to bring you to eternal life." Jude urges them to stay close to God, to pray, and to rely on the Holy Spirit to help them stay strong.

Jude also encourages them to show mercy and kindness to others, especially those who are struggling in their faith. He says, "Be merciful to those who doubt; save others by snatching them from the fire." While we must stand firm in the truth, we are also called to reach out with love and mercy to those who need help.

At the end of the letter, Jude offers a beautiful prayer. He praises God, saying, "To Him who is able to keep you from stumbling and to present you before His glorious presence without fault and with great joy—to the only God our Savior be glory, majesty, power, and authority, through Jesus Christ our Lord." Jude reminds the believers that God is able to keep them safe and strong, and that they can trust in His power to help them.

Jesus's Message to You...
There will be people who try to lead you away from Me, but remember to stay close to God's Word, pray, and rely on the Holy Spirit to help you. Show love and mercy to others, and never forget that I am with you, keeping you safe. You are Mine, and I will always guide you in My truth!

CHAPTER 66

REVELATION: THE VICTORY OF JESUS

The apostle John wrote a very special and exciting letter called Revelation. This letter is full of visions and messages from Jesus that show us what will happen at the end of time. Though it might be a little hard to understand, Revelation is a book full of hope, because it tells us that in the end, Jesus wins!

John begins the book by sharing how he received this message from Jesus.

He was on an island called Patmos when Jesus appeared to him and gave him a vision. In the vision, Jesus showed John what will happen in the future, and John was told to write it down and send it to seven churches. These churches were filled with believers who needed to hear the message of hope and warning that Jesus was giving.

Jesus told John about things that would happen, like the rise of powerful enemies who would try to hurt God's people. These enemies, called the beasts, would make it hard for people to follow Jesus. But Jesus promised that even though things might get tough, He would be with His people and would bring judgment on those who did wrong. He said that those who remain faithful to Him would receive great rewards, like being with Him forever in a new heaven and a new earth.

One of the most amazing things in Revelation is the picture of heaven.

John saw a vision of a beautiful place where there is no sadness or pain, where God lives with His people, and where everyone is worshiping Jesus. John says, "I saw a new heaven and a new earth, for the first heaven and the first earth had passed away." In this new world, there will be no more crying or sickness—everything will be made perfect.

Jesus also gave John a message of warning to the churches. Some churches were doing well, living out their faith, while others needed to repent and turn back to God. Jesus told them to be strong and to hold onto the truth. He reminded them that He is the Alpha and the Omega, the beginning and the end. He is in control of everything, and no matter how hard things might get, we can trust in His victory.

As the book continues, John sees incredible things—angels singing, the opening of seals, and the pouring out of bowls of judgment. But the most important message is that Jesus will return! He is coming again to make all things new and to defeat evil once and for all. The Bible ends with the promise that Jesus will make everything right and that He will bring us into His eternal kingdom. He says, "I am coming soon. Blessed is the one who keeps the words of the prophecy in this scroll."

At the very end of Revelation, Jesus tells us to remember that He is coming back, and that we should be ready. He says, "I am the Alpha and the Omega, the First and the Last, the Beginning and the End." Jesus will return to take His people to live with Him forever in a perfect place where there is no pain, no tears, and no more sin.

Jesus's Message to You...
Children, remember that I am the Alpha and the Omega, the beginning and the end. Though bad things may happen in this world, know that I will make everything right in the end. I am coming back, and I want you to be ready! Hold onto truth, trust in Me, and know that you will live with Me forever in a perfect place where all will be made new. I love you, and I will never leave you!

THE END